"For years, I worked with Dennis Lynch as we covered televised trials around the country. As a videographer, he tells a story through the camera lens but now, in Shooting Saddam, he displays a remarkable talent for storytelling through words. Shooting Saddam transports us to Baghdad and his life as a civilian in the Green Zone. Lynch takes us through the set-up of the makeshift Iraqi courtroom for the first televised trial in Iraq's history. We have an inside look at the war crimes trials of Saddam Hussein and his cohorts including the courtroom antics the camera couldn't pick up. Lynch strikes a proper balance between self-deprecating humor and the somber portrayal of a terrifying subject—the trial and death verdict of a tyrant."

—Beth Karas, legal analyst, former Court TV correspondent

"Dennis is the consummate storyteller with a keen eye for details and color that brings the tales he tells to life. Whether he is behind the camera in a courtroom or behind a desk with pen in hand, Dennis is always the seasoned professional with an uncanny ability to bring the reader or viewer along on the journey into the stories that have become, and will become, the history of our time."

—Brian Skoloff, journalist, author, "Killer Girlfriend: The Jodi Arias Story"

"Dennis is a fantastic cameraman and journalist that I had the pleasure to work with for many years at Court TV. He covered some of the great trials of our day from OJ Simpson and Scott Peterson to Michael Jackson and Phil Spector. Dennis is a consummate professional and always won over the court staff with his congenial personality. He has a nose for news and always got the intricate details right. When Dennis went to Baghdad to cover the trial of Saddam Hussein I had confidence that it would be covered professionally. I also knew Dennis would have a great story to tell when it was over."

—Tom Donohue, former Director of Assignments Court TV

"Don't let the title fool you. You are instantly fond of the storyteller and his bold humor. I found myself repeating one-liners out loud with a smile stretched across my face. What an incredible journey and a privilege to share it with Dennis Lynch."

—Kinsey Schofield, E! Channel Personality, and Social Media Savant

DISCARD

SHOOTING SADDAM

DENNIS LYNCH

TABLE OF CONTENTS

DEDICATION

*This book owes its existence to the help
and encouragement of numerous friends
and colleagues. I am especially compelled
to acknowledge and thank the following
people: Mitchell for providing the
opportunity; the RCLO Iraqi nationals
for generously offering their insight; Lisa
for pointing me in the right direction; Win
for believing in the story; Gregg Olsen for
making it happen; the beta readers for
suffering through an unedited manuscript;
my family for their enthusiasm and
support; and mostly, my wife Meredith.
Her patience and reassurance persevered
through my low points of procrastination,
and the excitement of completion. This
book is for her.*

About the Author

Since he began working with Court TV in1997, Dennis has been in the courtroom of nearly every high profile hearing or trial west of the Mississippi. Including Jodi Arias, O.J. Simpson's Las Vegas trial, Dr. Conrad Murray, Scott Peterson, Robert Blake, Ted Binion, Phil Spector, Noura Jackson, James Ray/Sweat lodge, Brandon Wilson/Matthew Cecchi,  David Westerfield/Danielle van Dam, Kobe Bryant, and Manson Family parole hearings.

The trials have been carried live on Court TV, In Session, HLN, CNN, and featured numerous times as main stories on *"Dateline," "48 Hours,"* and *"20/20."*

As a Director of Photography, Dennis has travelled extensively around the country filming documentaries, cable series, live events, and instructional programs for broadcast and corporate markets.

During his 38 years in film and television, Dennis and associated productions received numerous acknowledgements including the CINE Golden Eagle, Gold Cindy/IFPA, Angel and Halo, Film Advisory Board of Excellence, and Telly awards

Dennis Lynch graduated from Chapman University with a double major in English and Communications.

Dennis is currently working on a behind the scenes trial series including Jodi Arias, Phil Spector, Dr. Conrad Murray, and O.J. Simpson.

Introduction

Who better to tell the story of a monster's tyranny and outrageous, evil crimes than the man behind the camera—the guy there, every day, inside the courtroom, putting every single word, every accusation, every fact, every nightmare, into the world record on film?

When Dennis Lynch travelled to Iraq to film the trials of Saddam Hussein—images beamed all over the world so the rest of us could be there with him—he had already amassed considerable experience behind the camera with some of America's most infamous cases. Since he began working for Court TV in 1997, Lynch has seen and recorded just about every high-profile hearing or trial west of the Mississippi. All of us know the names: Jodi Arias, O.J. Simpson, Dr. Conrad Murray, Scott Peterson, Robert Blake, Ted Binion, Phil Spector, Kobe Bryant. When courtroom cameras weren't permitted, Lynch moved outside with the reporters for trials such as Warren Jeffs, Elizabeth Smart, O.J. Simpson's civil trial, Matthew Shepard, and Michael Jackson's pedophilia case.

As a Director of Photography, Dennis has travelled extensively while filming documentaries, cable series, live events, and instructional programs for broadcast and corporate markets. During his 38 years in film and television, Dennis and associated productions he worked for received numerous acknowledgements including the CINE Golden Eagle, Gold Cindy/IFPA, Angel and Halo, Film Advisory Board of Excellence, and Telly awards.

Thus, it comes as no surprise to us at Crime Rant Books that we run into Dennis Lynch as he publishes his first book, a behind-the-scenes narrative of the televised coverage of Saddam Hussein's trial, the monster of Iraq. The man we all hated and wanted to see punished for the atrocious crimes against humanity he perpetrated.

What happened in the hallways of the courtroom? What did some of the players talk about when the cameras weren't rolling? What are the true secrets U.S. government officials don't want to get out? How graphic and inhumane were Saddam's actual crimes?

Those are only a few of the many questions Dennis Lynch began asking himself as he decided to pen the story behind the story, the tale behind the horror.

Out of fear and perhaps boredom, Dennis Lynch looked for and found the offbeat side of the conflict while in Iraq: seeing troops wearing full battle gear over Santa costumes, hot days lounging around Saddam's pool with weapon-carrying soldiers in bathing suits, watching visiting Senator Joe Biden ignored and left standing alone, or Senator John Kerry roaming the dining hall trying to find someone interested in meeting him.

These stories tell us about the *people* behind the war, the players involved on a daily basis in the Iraq initiative that was causing so much dissolution of our political system back home.

Dennis participated in the hectic courtroom preparations, and during the trial he witnessed unreported proceedings and court behavior of Saddam Hussein and his co-defendants that has never been made public.

That is, until now, in Dennis Lynch's riveting, exclusive account of it all, *Shooting Saddam*.

Lynch not only takes the reader secretly behind the action of Saddam's trial, where reporters couldn't go, but directly into Saddam's holding cell, where readers meet the Devil behind all the evil himself. Shooting Saddam is a memoir wrapped in a thriller that is as offbeat and enlightening as it is alarming and revealing in ways you could never imagine.

If you wanted to know anything about the real Saddam Hussein, look no further—Dennis Lynch's account is all together one of the most revealing pieces of war reportage ever written.

—*New York Times* bestselling authors
M. William Phelps & Gregg Olsen,
Publishers, Crime Rant Books

Shooting Saddam

In late October 2005, I was working as a cameraman for Court TV, covering the wrongful death civil trial of Robert Blake in Burbank, California. Blake, the actor whose career spanned the *Little Rascals*, a sadistic killer in the movie *In Cold Blood*, and '70s badass cop Baretta, had been acquitted of murdering his psycho-wife, Bonnie Lee Bakley. I had been in the courtroom for most of the criminal trial proceedings, so Blake was familiar with seeing me around.

Since no cameras were allowed in the civil trial, I was at our outside position near where Robert Blake parked. Blake and I had a professional understanding. I gave him slack during court breaks and didn't shoot him in his car napping. In turn, Blake allowed me to get my required daily shots of him walking or standing around smoking.

At lunch, Blake entertained us with colloquialism-laced stories of old Hollywood and his glory years. He talked about tough times, being knocked down in life, and fashioned himself as an "old cowboy" who repeatedly climbed "back on the bull." One day our conversation turned to the more serious, current topic of the Iraq war. I told Blake I was leaving to cover Saddam Hussein's trial in a few weeks.

He did a double-take, and then barked, "Are you fucking nuts?" I hadn't really stopped to think of it like that. The exotic travel, doing something boastfully unique, and having steady work had blinded me.

But the crazy old cowboy was right. In a short time, I would find out I was nuts.

PART ONE

Chapter 1

Getting There

On the November 11, 2005 drive to Los Angeles International Airport, I am still trying to rationalize it in my head. My wife is proud of me, though she is worried about the dangers I will be facing. Since I'm not much of a talker, the awkward silence hides the fact I just feel numb. As a freelance cameraman, I occasionally work in uncomfortable or potentially dangerous situations, but for the most part, the biggest danger is craft services. Volunteering to work in a war zone is really different. I am joining seven television professionals, chosen for our production experience and apparent lack of common sense, to begin a remarkable trip to Baghdad, Iraq.

There, we'll televise the crimes against humanity trial of Saddam Hussein. My expertise is operating robotic cameras in high-profile criminal trials, and I am going to be directing the opening months of the proceedings broadcast to the world.

As I pass through the airport's final screening, my wife's teary eyes look frightened, and then she is gone from sight. Though apprehensive about my load of classified body armor, "I'm going to Iraq" seems to satisfy the TSA screener. I haven't had any coffee yet, so I make the first of my "last" stops at Starbucks. I know I am going to a land of barbarians who do not have one of my blessed sanctuaries in their entire country. My group somberly boards the plane for our next stop, a truly frightening place, foreign, full of violence and poverty—Detroit.

Holding firmly to my carry-on luggage through the Detroit airport, I reach the Royal Jordanian Airlines departure gate for Amman. Talk about feeling out of place. I am instantly struck by the fact I am now the foreigner and I haven't even left the U.S. (although I often feel that way in parts of Los Angeles). My fellow passengers are women with henna-dyed hands, dressed in traditional Islamic garb, accompanied by swarthy men in open shirts proudly displaying gold chains and poodle-hairy chests.

They are casually talking, not paying attention to me. Still, I am uneasy. Out of my comfort zone, and with all the profiling paranoia, I just hope the Patriot Act isn't correct in assuming everyone who looks different is packing lighters in their shoes. The mere fact I am going to Amman is reason enough to be worried. It has only been two days since the bombings of the Jordanian Grand Hyatt, Radisson, and Days Inn in Amman, killing fifty-seven people.

I am lucky to score a window seat. This is going to be a long flight, and I want to see the world go by, perhaps for the last time. I introduce myself to the kid sitting next to me. His name is Mohammed, and he is my first exposure to the Arabic language. When the flight attendants begin their safety demonstration, they sound annoyed with the passengers. I later come to understand that the Arabic language is very passionate, and theirs is just a normal conversational tone.

The flight is routine until the seat-belt sign turns off, and the passengers take literally the phrase "You are free to move about the cabin." The main cabin erupts as an airborne social gathering with the Detroit passengers changing seats, standing, hanging over seat backs, and talking. Some are praying in the aisles and in between rows. Others sleep on the floor. A woman startles the entire plane with horrific wailing. Flight attendants and nearby passengers rush to comfort her, but most of the Detroit passengers have no reaction at all. It freaks me out. Mohammed listens to the commotion and tells me that the woman dreamed her soul was being taken.

Oh, that? I get that feeling every April 15.

I manage to sleep or read during most of the flight. In the middle of the night we are served our dinner: traditional Arabic fare, hummus and fruits. I decline, and yearn for good old peanuts. Then things get worse, something shaming me as an American. The in-flight movie is the *Dukes of Hazzard* remake. Oh, the humiliation.

As our plane meets the rising sun, we pass over Europe and a glorious view of the Alps. I drift in and out of a restless nap, half waking over Greece, and then again when we start our descent at the Dead Sea. The landscape is barren and brown. Touching down in Jordan, I feel there must be some mistake. The abandoned-looking runway is bumpy and overgrown with weeds. Not a building in sight. The entire plane erupts in applause at our fortune in merely landing. With the grace of a Conestoga wagon traversing a dry creek bed, we arrive at the seedy Queen Alia airport in Amman.

As members of my group wrangle for entry permits and transfers, I notice a familiar and unexpected sight. Starbucks. I try to suppress a squeal of joy as I grab my next "last cup." Our television crew chief has to call the hotel and the embassy staff to get us through security. We are eventually "expedited" in about two hours. I don't care. I have coffee. The plan is to spend the night in Amman, and then leave next morning for Iraq. Some of my team waits in vain for luggage that never arrives, and probably never left Detroit.

Security is evident as my team boards the minibus to the hotel a mile away. The shades are drawn to hide our noticeably white American faces. Makeshift barricades made from large planter boxes border the hotel driveway in a lame attempt to prevent further bombings. In the dark we are let off on the road, away from the hotel. Our driver directs us to a dimly lit search area in the driveway, where our bags will be opened and scrutinized. The guards seem particularly interested in the one female crewmember and her luggage contents. Another search area awaits us in the hotel lobby.

Once inside, the hotel staff tells us if we had just tipped the guards we could have bypassed the enhanced security searches. I guess a guy wearing a natty explosive vest and handing out five bucks can waltz through.

The Alia Hotel probably saw its glory years during the Carter Administration. But it is still a charming step back in time. I am actually glad to discover the hotel and airport are twenty-some miles from Amman. The further from recent bomb targets the better. Our group is famished, so we make our way to the hotel restaurant. Depending on how you look at it, I guess I'm lucky the menu has English descriptions so I can make the difficult culinary decision between lamb-this and lamb-that. Between the flight meal and this dinner,

I am well on my way to losing some weight. The hotel, lobby, and shops are quiet and mostly empty. Yet, I am surprised how little attention we draw from the few locals hanging around. It's almost like other Americans have come before us. It will be a long day tomorrow, so I make a quick call home for five dollars a minute, buy some nonsensical trinkets in the gift shop, and then head up to my room to watch Arabic soap operas.

The next morning brings more security issues. Some crewmembers have to pay hundreds of dollars for "overweight" baggage. A scam for sure, but we aren't the ones holding the guns, so we can do nothing but fork over the cash. The Jordanian soldiers also refuse to let us fly with our body armor. As the guards sit around smoking cigarettes with an indifference to our fate, our crew leader pulls out a U.S. Embassy letter stating how "important" we are and how we must travel with armor.

In reality, we can't even get off the plane in Baghdad without armor. With the full weight of a generic photocopied letter, we are finally allowed to proceed to the gate, fortuitously adjacent to the Starbucks. With fresh nectar in hand, I go through additional security to enter a special holding room for the Baghdad passengers. Rejoice, other Americans! The room is filled with really big, really rugged gun-for-hire Americans, with arms the size of Virginia hams. Chatting, laughing and calm, they must be back from holiday.

I surmise they talking about us, and wondering what a bunch of nervous wimps are doing on this flight.

At this time, Royal Jordanian Airlines operates the only commercial flight to Baghdad. Holding twenty-some passengers, it is an unmarked white jet, supposedly with British Airways pilots. From Amman, the short flight to Baghdad has a reputation for being interesting. Once we enter Iraqi airspace I feel like the pilots are either wrestling in the cockpit, or traversing an obstacle course. With hard banks to the left and right, we're told the serpentine moves make it harder for insurgents to hit a weaving target. The finale of the flight is a tight corkscrew descent that can make people sick.

Most of the airport is closed, while a portion of Baghdad International Airport remains open to special arrivals. For the first time in months it is raining in Saddam's land. Surrounding the immediate tarmac outside our plane are lots of serious guys sporting serious guns. Out-of-service Iraqi airliners are pulled up to dormant gates for passengers that will never come. As our group enters the terminal, our escort, a U.S. Army captain, takes us through Iraqi security.

The once-stylish terminal interior is eerily silent with unoccupied gates, vacant shops, and empty restaurants. Some stores still have merchandise, like the owners just locked the door one day and never came back. Near an inactive baggage carousel, there's a group of Iraqi men hanging around waiting for their fortunes to change.

As I exit the terminal, its exterior shows signs of decay and war. Dangling wires hang from the ceiling, rocks and concrete blocks litter the road, and crumbling walls once accented by landscape, have fallen victim to weeds. There are only a handful of passengers being picked up today. Waiting just for us are three SUVs, and Humvees with armed U.S. soldiers.

We feel like celebrities.

Shortly after we exit the airport area, our lead driver misses a crucial turn and suddenly places us on the business side of Abrams tanks sitting sentinel in the road. Our environment is instantly barbed wire and desolation. There is no mistaking this stretch of highway as the infamous Route Irish. We are on the most dangerous road in the world in broad daylight.

Not wanting to embarrass myself in front of the attractive female soldier driving my vehicle, I silently scream "U turn! U turn!" Our convoy quickly scampers back on to friendly soil to make our first stop at Camp Victory, site of one of Saddam's tributes to himself and home to U.S. Army command. The impressive Qasr al Fao Palace sits next to a gigantic man made lake that's surrounded by massive guest homes.

Camp Victory is a small city with rumbling convoys, soldiers casually walking roads with American street names, and fast-food outlets. High above the camp are balloons that resemble small blimps. I am told these triangulate incoming projectiles, and a response can often hit the insurgents before they have a chance to get away. You have to love that stuff.

As night falls, our escort rounds up some spare DFAC meals of fried scallops, crab legs, steak and fries. DFAC stands for Dining Facility, one of the many acronyms popular with the military. There aren't enough meals for us all, and though we are starving, we behave like grown-ups and share. Since we are on hold until we move to our next location, the captain tells us we are welcome to use the driving range. Enterprising soldiers constructed a tee on our building's roof, and supplied it with clubs and tons of balls. In the spirit of a brash occupying force, several of us whack away into the black lake until we are offered a trip to the PX.

We learn misplaced or unattended bags never arrive in Baghdad, and the unfortunate must wait for them outside the country. Once in Iraq, any hope of retrieving clothes is gone. Some of our crew have been wearing the same delicates for a couple of days, and desperately need to go shopping to replace lost underwear and socks.

After eating, golf, and shopping, it is time to go the staging area at Camp Stryker, where we meet our transport to the Green Zone. Even though it's late at night, there is plenty of activity. Harsh generator lights illuminate rows of parked military vehicles surrounding the area. The air is filled with the constant convoy drone of Humvees and supply trucks. Our meeting area is a plywood shack encased with sandbags called the "Stables." The rain mixing with the talcum-like dust is manufacturing Iraq's infamous muck, which should be marketed as industrial glue. This stuff sticks to everything, and the more you try to get it off, the more it spreads.

Inside the shack, I am greeted with a hot, stuffy funk that only a bunch of men can create. There are two help desks; one for transport, and the other for billeting. There is no sleeping allowed in the building, so people either get a bunk, or stay in the room of zombies. One side has a stack of M-rations; the other side features tables and chairs. Toward the rear are vinyl couches, romance novels, and a big-screen television. Every conceivable space is jammed with packs, suitcases, and guns. There is coffee, but it tastes like Colin Powell brewed it during the Gulf War.

This is the first time I have the opportunity to place my ceramic plates into my flak vests and put my helmet on. The gear is going to be required for the trip into Baghdad, and I want to look battle-ready. After seeing soldiers look so cool wearing this stuff, I feel like such a nerd. As we take pictures, everyone in our group fortunately looks dorky too. An accessory to the protective vest is a crotch protector, able to withstand small-arms fire. It dangles precariously like a limp beaver's tail. My vanity overrides my sense of safety and I decline.

Departure times for convoys are a secret. We are given a travel-time window, and that is it. The convoy travels twice a night between the Green Zone and Camp Victory. Depending on their progress and any unforeseen events, the military leaves plenty of time to reach the destination. After hearing the roads have been cleared (cleared of what, I don't want to know), we are told to prepare to load our bags. Bags are lined up and stacked in the mud. Everyone forms a line to help pitch the bags in the trucks. Within minutes, the mud rapidly mutates and attacks the luggage and anyone touching them. (To this day, some of my bags still have remnants of that night, and those bags made the journey to Iraq three times.)

We are directed to a row of what looks like black Winnebago motor homes. These are the Rhino Runners, advertised as the most impervious vehicle on the planet. Dealer options include darkened windows of bulletproof glass, hatches on the bottom and top, gun ports in each row, and school bus seating inside.

Each Rhino has a U.S. Marshal as a spotter, and twenty-three passengers. We are given brief instructions on what to do should we be attacked, or get blown over by a roadside bomb: Just get out, stay down and push the Rhino back right-side.

It is cold, dark, I'm tired, and this is getting scary.

A small contingent of Humvees forms the head and tail of the convoy. Over the radio a marshal keeps calling "Halo, Halo," and I soon surmise he is either communicating with a helicopter escort above, or looking for heavenly guidance. We are told there is no air cover available tonight, so hopefully angels answered. Along the route are hidden U.S. soldiers and Quick Response Units of Humvees, should any Iraqis not welcome our tourist dollars. Our Marshal uses night-vision binoculars, wary of things I can't see and surely don't want to know about.

Along Route Irish, the perilous main road from the airport to the city, the lights around houses only break the darkness. Most use fluorescent shop lights that display plain box-like buildings, scattered junk, and absolutely no sense of landscaping design. We reach a checkpoint about half way into Baghdad. Dull amber lights reveal a stark, sandbag-and barbed-wire outpost. A small guard tower oversees the entire area. A camouflaged bunker, protruding the barrel of a 50-caliber machine gun, sits firmly in the middle of the road. I can't imagine being stationed in the harshness of that kind of nowhere. It takes special people to man a post so isolated, dangerous, and exposed.

Our bus ride eventually enters winding, dimly lit city streets. The ambient glow from the city silhouettes massive government buildings bordered by blast walls. We pull into a heavily guarded walled complex. At 5 a.m., our embassy escort is there to greet us. Grabbing our belongings, we pile into an armored Suburban. Dawn is breaking as we drive across the street to another checkpoint at the entrance of Saddam's Republican Palace.

Chapter 2

My New Home

Knowing this place from television, but never expecting to visit, it's surreal that by chance I am here. Walking up the driveway the enormity of the building is staggering. The palace features a huge dome in the middle section, with two massive wings on either side. The wings have covered porticos with dramatic Ba'ath emblems of stern-looking falcons, reminiscent of Nazi décor. The walls are etched with Saddam's signature and pithy quotes. I'm guessing not *My home is your home*. The palace lawn features a kitschy fountain and pool with a griffin emerging from water spouting fish. Since the owner is in the pokey, the fountain is turned off.

Near the front entrance stands another idle fountain, an immense, ugly golden spiked ball. Like a Hollywood party, parked along the drive is a fleet of armored Suburban and Mercedes SUVs. We continue through several more checkpoints, which are located at each building and area entrance, every couple hundred of yards within the embassy compound. Private guards from contractor Triple Canopy man these internal checkpoints. Most of the guys are from Central and South America, and speak very little English.

Being from Southern California, I feel right at home.

Upon entering the round foyer, the floor is marble, and the ceiling opens up to the dome. A large carpet hangs from the wall, hiding some tile work Saddam had done that the U.S. command finds offensive. On a table sits a broken architect's model of the palace.

Nestled in an alcove are chairs left over from the regime. Of course, we have to sit in them, imagining who has sat there before. The upholstery is velvet, gaudy material with gold arms and legs. The tile work along the walls and ceiling are intricate designs with pastel colors. Hanging in the halls are numerous chandeliers. Saddam reveled in this splendor as his people starved. And this is just one of the many palaces that dot the city and country within an easy drive from one another.

As we wait, and wait, waiting to get told what to do, we look more closely. The ceiling tile work is made of preformed sections, the lights are tarnished brass, and the chandelier "glass" is plastic. The chairs are poorly painted and the marble floors aren't laid out straight. At first glance it all appears opulent; up close, it's ridiculous. The Republican Palace looks more like a movie set than a show place for Saddam's events. But then, Saddam did not fear criticism.

After being up for well over twenty-four hours, we are taken to billeting to get our room assignments. Military contractors KBR (Kellogg, Brown, Root) have built numerous portable buildings on the backside of the palace to function as housing, post office, billeting, DFAC, etc. Stepping out the back of the palace there is a little tree-lined street with old-fashioned street lamps. It sort of reminds me of Main Street at Disneyland, minus the whole "The Happiest Place on Earth" thing. Even at daybreak there are soldiers and contractors busily going somewhere, and a frightening number of birds and bats in the trees.

The housing is divided into homey-sounding sections like "Edgewood," "Embassy Suites," and

"Riverfront." They are composed of two portable trailers, about ten feet by twenty feet, two people to a side, with a bathroom in the middle. Between the hundreds of trailers stand rows of sandbags ten feet tall. There are cement bunkers that are more like open boxes, located conveniently nearby. If a mortar hits in the vicinity, it will probably only prevent blood from splattering everywhere.

I am assigned a trailer with a stranger, and arriving with all my stuff at dawn doesn't seem to sit well with my sleepy new roommate. He grumbles something and turns over. By this time, the dining hall is opening so my ragged crew heads off, since we haven't really eaten all day.

Our military will never starve. Every base meal is like an all-you-can-eat Las Vegas buffet. The DFAC has it all; any kind of omelet is made to order, and there are pancakes, sausages, fruit, and a sandwich bar. I wish to express gratitude to the American taxpayer for enabling me to eat so well.

We are given about an hour to rest before we have to start the credential process, and I meet my roommate. Plastered all over his wall are naked photos of his girlfriend. I guess he wasn't expecting company. Our crew has been emphatically warned not to discuss our purpose in Iraq. Besides making me feel like a secret agent, it also appears rude when the guy asks me what I do. I have to defer, even though there are a lot of people doing more secret stuff, probably him included. He seems a bit put off, like he can tell I am just a new kid in camp. By the time I get back that night, he has moved out and I never see him again. His half of the trailer is larger, so I move to his side even though he has taken all the photos.

I spend the entire day unpacking, getting credentials, getting my corneas photographed in the basement of the parliament building, and generally being led around on a field trip by our handler. The schedule doesn't allow for the eleven-hour jet lag and lack of sleep, so I ignore it. This is my first daylight exposure to the (International) Green Zone.

The "International" name conjures up a coalition; to make everyone think there is progress and it is safer. Those that are here call it the Green Zone, or "IZ." On the sightseeing tour, I see the sights familiar to all who watched the U.S. night bombing on television: huge, lavish government buildings all sharing the characteristic massive holes punched in them by smart bombs. The structures are mostly still usable, but Defense Secretary Donald Rumsfeld sent the eviction notice to get out. Still standing undisturbed are the Crossed Swords at the parade ground, the Tomb of the Unknowns, convention center and parliament buildings, the Al Rasheed hotel, and surrounding neighborhoods.

There are still Iraqis living in the area. Most are modest homes and all have walls around them. Various foreign interests now occupy the larger homes that once housed Saddam's favorite henchmen. Armed guards stand out in the streets amongst the stray dogs and skeletons of exploded cars. The Iraqi women walking around in abayas make for a stark contrast to the occasional infidel jogger or biker. A few Iraqi vendors brave the open street corners, selling handbags and t-shirts.

The streets are dirty and lined with broken concrete and blast walls. Discouraged policemen stand in the middle of traffic circles waving at speeding dilapidated cars that pay little attention to them. The military convoys ignore traffic control outright. The color of Baghdad—the houses, and ground, even the sky—is beige. The date palms all have a layer of Mesopotamian dust and just look tired of living. When planning a vacation, skip the "Cradle of Civilization" tour during times of war.

After getting our eyes and background checked, we cross the street to the Al Rasheed (or Rashid) hotel, famous as CNN's outpost during the Gulf War. The Rasheed is now well protected and secure (sporting its own guard tower and armed guards) after insurgents brazenly fired rockets from a park across the street.

The hotel features a small mall of vendors that sell Rolex knockoffs, rugs, videos, knives, and lots of junk souvenirs. I pick up a really cool lighter for five dollars that has portraits of Saddam and President Bush, with a fighter jet on top. When lit, the sound of a bomb plays. The hotel entrance floor has a tile portrait that offers patrons a chance to walk on former President George H.W. Bush and show disdain. The street dividing the hotel and the convention center leads to a Red Zone gate a few hundred feet away. It gives me the creeps being that close, like standing near a ledge, thinking someone is going to push. We are warned to not walk in a group, but spread out when in the open or crossing the road.

In the morning I see Iraqis line up outside the embassy compound to come to work: older men wearing suit pants and dress shirts, younger men wearing sports warm-ups, others in traditional garb. All are just grateful to have jobs. The workers are hand-searched coming and going. They clean the palace, the trailer bathrooms, and maintain the grounds. (For the most part, landscaping is just sweeping the dust from one place to another). A Green Zone job creates risks for the workers. If insurgents find out about a worker, the worker and/or family will be killed.

Some of the nationals cast wary eyes; some smile and say hello. But they seem to have been instructed not to associate with us. I find them all polite. As in any government workplace, you have the hard workers, and then the guys who lean on mops. There are Iraqi women, generally younger, that do not work out in the residence areas, but inside the palace. After the long day of work, the Iraqis grab lots of precious bottled water before they exit the gate. Water is a scarce commodity in today's Baghdad.

Throughout the day, calls to prayer echo across the city. It seems so exotic, except they start at five in the morning. For me, it is an indicator to go eat. While we wait for our chance to get over to the courthouse for the first time, we familiarize ourselves with the PX area and some of the local vendors. There is a Burger King, Subway, pizza, and a coffee place named Blossoms. With the deluxe spread over at the DFAC, I never can understand eating at those places, but there are always a line of soldiers waiting for their Whoppers. The PX has pretty much anything you might need, such as clothing, electronics and toiletries. There are occasional shortages when supply convoys can't get through, or have been blown up. It is kind of hard to understand complaints about not having shampoo when somebody lost their life, but there are.

The hardest thing to get used to is the constant noise. There are massive generators powering the compound that sound and look like a herd of locomotives. Blackhawk helicopters land at the heliport across from the palace ferrying soldiers in and out all day. There is the buzzing of "Little Bird" helicopters with a bunch of armed Blackwater security guys hanging out the sides quickly passing overhead. Jets streak across the sky, and unseen drones hover like lazy hawks. Convoys returning from patrol blast sirens to clear the streets of traffic. The Medevac helicopters arriving every twenty minutes, twenty-four hours a day, flying low and fast to the hospital across the street make you feel sick that there are so many wounded. We learn six Americans have died on our first day in Baghdad.

Explosions are a common occurrence. For the most part they happen across the Tigris River, but feel like next door. You can often feel the concussion from a long ways away. Bombs are not something you get used to, but you learn to just go about your business. There is a predictable routine of explosions followed by the quick ramping up of helicopters.

Of course, the insurgents try to hit the embassy compound. There is such a helpless feeling in waking to the whistle of mortars. Or when walking in some open space and the shrill warning sirens go off. *"Duck and cover, duck and cover. Incoming!"* blasts over the speakers. And the best you can find for cover is one of those stupid cement boxes.

I usually try to make my way to the palace, where they have coffee and thick walls. The insurgents sneak down by the river to fire their mortars so they can be close enough to hit something. They usually step the mortars in as they find their range, presumably with the help of someone inside the IZ. All along the river side of the compound are guard towers, and the guards pick off the insurgents that expose themselves too much. Katyusha rockets are another problem. They can be launched from a rooftop or back of a pickup, and the insurgents disappear in minutes. Around five feet long and six inches around, the rockets aren't accurate, but pack a much bigger punch, and they sound scarier flying overhead. When those bad boys hit, you know it; you can feel it in your chest.

After being out of touch for a couple of days, I am finally able to make a short call home to let my wife know I am okay. The battery on our satellite phone is dying and the charger is in one of the crew's lost luggage. It is not the easiest thing to be that far away, be in a dangerous area, and do the "Hi Honey. I'm fine. Love you. Bye" thing. Until we get our own phones, there are state-side phones available in the embassy. Located in a room Saddam had decorated with a mural of SCUD missiles firing off to Iran, and charging horses on the ceiling dome, a bank of phones and computers provide a link back home. A line typically forms to get a precious call home that is limited to about ten minutes. I always feel guilty waiting ahead of the soldiers, so I keep my calls short.

Lines form for the computers as well, but we are provided with access to State Department computers. Calls and email are carefully monitored, as evidenced by some rather inflammatory remarks about Saddam that someone sent to me. That person ended up being blocked from receiving messages, or sending to my account. Not that I minded, as the last thing I wanted was to be called in as some threat to court security. In time, even more computers and printers are brought into the coffee shop. In order to stay within the time constraints, the trick is to write on your personal computer, put the message on a thumb drive, then transfer it when you get there. The connections are painfully slow, but a true luxury.

We have our own post office located on embassy grounds. Packages being sent out have to be inspected first for contraband. Things like souvenir butane lighters are not permitted, but a foot-long knife is okay. Once the package is checked and sealed, normal domestic postal rates apply. Express shipping is not an option, but packages only take about a week. Letters are free, so that is a bonus. Packages that arrive from home are in remarkably good shape. Domestic carriers back home can't safely ship from one town to another, but the military can ship a box of cookies from halfway around the world and not break one.

In a few days we get our own government-issued phones that allow us to call within the IZ, and we are able to get incoming calls from the U.S. The phone numbers are based in the States, which makes calling Iraq an easy long-distance call. These phones are another generous benefit that our soldiers do not enjoy. In most places, the soldiers have to buy expensive calling cards, or find a courtesy phone. Either way requires waiting in long lines.

The only restriction: We can't talk about where we are exactly, or what we are doing. This doesn't sit too well with my wife when she hears of some recent attacks and wants to know my proximity. She presses: "Are you near Camp Dragon, are you near Camp…?" The line goes dead. She calls back, more than a little ticked off ("Why did you hang up on me?"), and though I try to explain the limitations, she is not one to be satisfied with generalities, and continues asking questions.

Whoever is monitoring must have had enough, because the line goes dead again, and there are no more calls for a while. I learn that calls and emails on my state department account are in fact, listened to and watched. From then on, explosions during a phone conversation are described as "Yeah that was one, but not close," or "I've got to take cover."

Chapter 3

The Who, What, and Why

Our sponsoring department is the Regime Crimes Liaison's Office (RCLO). The RCLO has support staff comprising nearly one hundred and forty attorneys, investigators from the FBI, DEA, ATF, and USMS, forensic archeologists and pathologists, civilian contractors, and Iraqi nationals. All have the same task: assist the Iraq High Tribunal (IHT) to prosecute Saddam Hussein and his co-defendants for crimes against humanity. An American liaison appointed by the U.S. Attorney General heads the office. He works in conjunction with a military officer who is his chief of staff. The RCLO is affiliated with the departments of Justice, Defense, and State.

Established in 2004 by National Security Presidential Directive 37, the RCLO is tasked with developing an independent, transparent judiciary for the upcoming trials. Its work includes educating and training the judges on international human rights law, excavating and interpreting mass graves, court construction, and locating and transporting witnesses. Behind the scenes of the proceedings are many professionals who risk their lives to assist the IHT administration in conducting a fair and just trial.

Twelve-hour days are common for the RCLO embassy office staff of around twenty people. It seems that they are always at their desks, and I'm not sure any of them had many days off. Next door are Iraqi nationals who work as interpreters and translators. Despite exposing themselves and their families to substantial danger, these brave Shi'a, Sunni, and

Christian nationals come in every day; many face direct death threats, others keep their jobs secret from their loved ones. The Iraqi members of the RCLO are also kind and grateful. Despite having their world torn apart, and their lives in turmoil, they gladly sit and talk about their country and culture.

The Iraqi High Tribunal (IHT) began in December 2003, when the Iraqi Governing Council established what was then called the Supreme Iraqi Criminal Tribunal. It was later renamed the Iraqi Special Tribunal, and then finally named the Iraqi High Tribunal. The parliament actually changed the name again to the Iraqi High Criminal Court, but by that time nobody cared and continued to call it the IHT. The Coalition Provisional Authority (CPA) authorized the Iraqi provision for a court to try criminals of the former regime. Shortly after the transfer of sovereignty, the Iraqi Interim Government and Iraqi National Assembly amended and affirmed the statute to authorize the trial of citizens and residents of Iraq for crimes against humanity, genocide, and a host of other crimes between 1968-2003, when the Ba'athists were in power.

The IHT aspires to delegate justice based on Iraqi law and customs, with the legitimacy of internationally recognized legal standards and practices. The IHT is not an international court; the judges are Iraqi nationals drawn from across the country, and confirmed by two governing bodies. The tribunal conducts court in the Iraqi inquisitorial tradition, meaning the defendants themselves question the witnesses, frequently make statements, and address the judge. Even the judges examine the witnesses. The American adversarial tradition places more responsibility on the attorneys, the defendant remains mostly silent, and the judge quietly presides over the trial.

The boisterous nature and unfamiliar Iraqi protocol are a shock and disappointment for observers expecting American-style justice. But that is the point: This is not American justice. This trial needs to show the Iraqi people that a dictator who had brutalized their country can be brought to justice, and can receive a fair trial. It needs to show that the country has moved on and is rebuilding. Iraq is looking to the future, and punish those who compromised its past. It is supposed to create a shock wave across the region.

Saddam would have never allowed a trial system that afforded defendants so many rights, especially under international guidelines. In fact, Saddam forbade attorneys from traveling abroad to study international law. For this reason, judges and attorneys need the support and resources of the RCLO. Training in international legal concepts began in Iraq, and moved to The Hague, London, and Italy. The Iraqi judges were able to meet and learn from jurists conducting current and past crimes-against-humanity tribunals. They were given guidance and instruction by the world's leading authorities on international criminal law and human rights. The IHT is not a court designed to invoke the will of American interests, nor is it bound by American law.

Wearing full protective gear, our team makes our first run to the secret courthouse. No one is to know its location, what it is, or what we are doing. We are told in no uncertain terms that we cannot share what we do or see until the trials are over. Our initial information is that the court is within walking distance, but this is just misdirection. We head off through the morning commute, whizzing amongst traffic coming in fresh from the bridge that feeds from the Red Zone. Nervous drivers in speeding little cars and flatbed trucks filled with Iraqi workers try to negotiate the July 14th Monument traffic circle.

Our armored Suburban blasts through this cyclone with an arrogance that makes me proud to be part of the "Conquerors." Our civilian drivers yield to no one who isn't military. They will drive with one hand, and open their door and point a gun with the other if an Iraqi's car is driving too close.

After the circle of fun, we proceed down a wide boulevard bordered by rundown walled estates, and modest homes. A small store stands outside a guarded apartment complex. The store, with its barbecue out front, will become a familiar sight, and the final resting place of many a cloven-footed beast.

An Abrams tank in the middle of the road guards an opening in the blast walls that leads to a checkpoint manned by Iraqis. The guards nervously finger tap their AK-47s as they search the vehicle's exterior. We just as nervously hold up our embassy badges and proceed through a maze of blast walls. Next is a series of gates, and a large archway, before we come face to face with a gigantic building. The secret courthouse, we are informed, is inside the former Ba'ath party headquarters. The irony that Saddam will face trial in this building is not lost. Even better, Saddam will not know where the trial is for a long time. He will be blindfolded for the trip from Camp Cropper near the airport, and not recognize the newly renovated areas in the building.

The seven-story limestone monument to brutality has an ornate front of golden medallions, dramatic arches, and the biggest doors I've ever seen. On top is a partially reconstructed dome and idle cranes. The dome had been undergoing reconstruction since its destruction in the Gulf War. Then it was pounded again during Iraqi Freedom. Sorry.

The courthouse occupies the front section of the building. Most of the rest of the structure is too damaged from a precision bomb. There are plans to move the civilians working on the trial from the embassy to this building sometime during the trials. I'm just getting comfortable in my trailer, and the food is great. I don't want to move. Then there are also plans to move to the new embassy, but it's not expected to be completed until a year or so after its target date. Welcome to government contracts and the Middle East.

While the courthouse section has two sets of elevators, it is not advisable to take them if you want to be back for dinner, so we walk the stairs. Walking Iraqi stairs takes concentration, since the steps are uneven. It's something like getting your sea legs; once you get the hang of it, they are not a problem unless you are drinking coffee. The building is not ventilated and dusty, with construction occurring on every floor. The first floor has a lobby, where they are putting in small offices. The second floor is split, with the media room and the Internal Security Office Command (ISOC). The third floor is for the prosecutor's offices. The fourth floor houses the court, judicial chambers, and defense offices.

The fifth floor is our little piece of paradise. The sixth floor is being prepared for expansion, and the seventh is too damaged from bombs.

Since this area is pretty much left untouched, the seventh is the most interesting of the floors, and provides access to the roof. We have to go up to check the viability of microwaving our signal across town to the convention center. The broadcast of the trial is not going to be allowed from the site because of security. It is mandated that satellite uplinks occur away from the trial, to prevent a media circus outside the court building. Up the dark, uneven steps we proceed to a bomb-damaged room. Wires and light fixtures hang precariously from what's left of the ceiling. Parts of the wall are collapsed, and steel ladders to an upper roof are twisted.

As I walk toward the roof access door, I stop to look behind a curious metal door, and run into an American sniper. Turns out, this is his post, behind that door. He proudly shows our team the smart-bomb crater that caved in the center of the building. He cautions us to keep moving, stay low and not be in the open too long as we survey the roof area. It is our first exposure to true vulnerability. On the upper roof, up above us, is a sniper nest with an unlimited view of the surrounding area, a postcard panorama of Baghdad. To our left are the Crossed Swords, in front an apartment complex, to the right the new embassy construction within easy mortar range of the Tigris. There is also a water treatment plant that Saddam provided to the privileged few as the rest of the city suffered in drought. The preventative ducking and moving like a drunken monkey gets tiring and feels silly, so by the time we finish our survey, we are standing around taking photos to send back home.

We are not yet aware there are Iraqi insurgent spotters in the nearby apartment complex.

The inside stairway activity is a miracle of human endurance. Dozens of Iraqis are marching up and down the flights like ants on a mission, carrying whatever is asked of them, hour after hour. Bags of cement, large office furniture; construction materials goes up, debris goes down. Most odd are the bags of dirt coming from the fourth floor. For some reason, a huge section of that floor level contains dirt, lots of it. It had to have been brought up at some time, and now, it is going back to rejoin Mother Earth.

I look in the room of the source, and it seems possible to have planted corn in there. Once removed, flooring is put in so the defense can have a nice, big lounge. But, even as we run cables from floor to floor, there is dirt in the crawl spaces between floors. We learn Saddam has done something interesting with this building: It is a building within a building. The exterior shell of limestone is separated by about a two-foot gap from the concrete and brick structure within. Dirt was placed between floors as a buffer. The building could take a mortar attack from some of Saddam's less loyal subjects, and not disturb the torture festivities the Ba'ath party had planned for the day.

Our fifth floor is the challenge. Within two weeks we need to turn an empty, dust-filled open space into a working control room. The entire courthouse facility will have to be wired for video feeds from the cellblock in the basement, to the counsel offices, media area, security room, and the court room itself. There are no professional supply outlets, so all the cables and connections have to be custom-made on site.

The courtroom floor really is composed of two stories. Rumored to have once been a trophy room for Saddam, its walls and floors are marble, and the elevated ceiling has chandeliers. The room has been undergoing reconstruction since before we arrived. Though the room was used for the initial hearing on October 16, the room does not reflect how the Iraqis or our government want the court to look.

The entire rear of the room has two levels of bulletproof-tinted glass viewing windows. The top level is designated the VIP area; the bottom is for the media. Large curtains are pulled back for viewing, but can, and will be closed, as the judge sees fit. The curtains will be drawn closed as the defendants enter, and will open once the judges are satisfied there is a reasonable possibility of order in the court.

Also part of the setup are the translation rooms. Some of the judges and witnesses speak Kurdish, so there are Kurdish-to-Arabic, Kurdish-to-English, and Arabic-to-English translators. Below them is the media support room where the prosecution prepares their evidence presentations. A pool still photographer will also be located there, with remote access to two still cameras, one above the judges' entry, and the other hidden directly behind the bench.

The counsel tables and court bench are covered in plastic sheeting as we enter. Busy Iraqi workers are painting, plastering, and sawing. The rickety two-story scaffolding is moved by hand as work slowly progresses. The Iraqis work hard and fast, but not efficiently. I watch them reapply plaster and paint over already completed areas. There's lots of long heated discussions with lots of pointing. Where sections of drywall shows large gaps in the joints, the workers simply tape it over, add some plaster, and paint it.

Since the electrical outlets and extension cords are a hodgepodge of European, Middle Eastern, and Edison formats, the workers snip and strip the end of the tool wires, and plug the exposed copper into whatever outlet they can find. With all the bare hands, sandaled feet and live wiring, I am surprised no one gets electrocuted. The Iraqis are masters of improvisation when it comes to utilizing what they have. During construction in our room, I witness a most amazing power saw-turned into a table saw combination. The saw is bolted upside down with the blade facing up between two boards. The ingenious device works like a champ.

But like the palace, nothing is constructed for longevity, or by any modern building codes.

The defendants' cage, where Saddam and his cohorts will sit, is divided into three sections, each with its own gate. Originally, the wrought-iron bars were painted white, but drew criticism for looking like a baby's crib (a metaphor that will later seem prophetic). As workers scurry around in the haze of pulverized drywall and sawdust, a new layer of oil-based paint is applied. It must be from the "Ugliest Brown Collection," and draws even less favorable comparisons. After the fumes have sapped a couple of year's memories from everyone, a nice redwood color is applied. Ah, just right.

The aesthetics and political proprieties are something to behold. The next issue to try men's souls is the platform height from which the trial participants will operate. In Iraqi courts, you just don't stand on the floor; everyone has a level of hierarchy. The defendants have a platform that can't be higher than the witness platform. The defense has a platform that has to match their podium platform, and it can't be higher than the prosecution. Of course, the prosecution can't be higher than the judges' platform.

The RCLO chief of staff in charge of this construction mess is a Navy captain who has the misfortune of having a background in engineering. His job is the proverbial "herding cats." On the eve of the impending crimes-against-humanity trial, he has to make several trips to dangerous Red Zone courthouses to verify and measure the average heights of platforms. This petty detail is a huge deal to the Iraqis. Platforms are built, then rebuilt, and rebuilt again. As Iraq's first televised trial, everything has to be just so.

After we've been here a week, the last of our six pallets of equipment arrive. Included in this shipment is my main suitcase. Thinking my bag will be safer sent in a bulk load than on our commercial flight, I gamble and win. Initially, our government offers to be helpful and provide equipment transportation on military aircraft. After all, they have direct flights without customs, and we are working for them. But, instead of using a plane that is going to Iraq anyway, the government decides it is a better use of taxpayer dollars to pay huge commercial fees to ship essential equipment that may or may not arrive in time.

So, our crew chief has to find the next best alternative, which I think has our equipment tour the entire Middle East by camel caravan before arriving. As we walk out to meet the flatbed truck, the enormity of our task sets in. Or maybe it is all the flights of stairs these boxes have to go up. Then like a guardian angel, the friendly courthouse project manager appears, and offers the assistance of some hapless Iraqi workers to do the heavy lifting.

Without hesitation, the workers start heaving stuff on their backs that I wouldn't put in a pickup truck. Up and down the hot, stuffy stairwell: "Yes, that's good, right over there, no, maybe over there." Life is good. Now if they know how to set up cameras, I can go back to the embassy and have lunch.

We may be content to have others do our work, but we are gracious, and we offer the workers water and snacks. The bribes work until we get a reprimand by our RCLO handler for being nice. "The workers are not to be trusted," we are told. In fact, we have to hide our photo badge should insiders try to get our name, or see the badge to duplicate it. When a curious Iraqi starts asking our names and where we are from, he is reported and reassigned. Obviously, there isn't a lot of confidence in the worker-vetting process. At this point, we are too tired to be alarmed. We head back to comfort of the DFAC, a meeting, and our beds.

There are lots of meetings. By now the time difference is taking its toll. Our group just sits blurry-eyed as people take their turn outlining logistic and security details, attending new hire orientations, and reminding us that President Bush is monitoring what we are doing. We are after all, there under his presidential directive. Sounds impressive, but I'll trade it for a shower and lying horizontal.

Our exhaustion doesn't deaden the concussion of explosions. One nearby car bomb kills twelve. The occurrence of bombs and gunfire never lets you truly rest. Following alerts, the M*A*S*H-sounding embassy address system comes on and explains what just happened. Sometimes the explosions sound like a distant construction job dropping large objects; others smack your ears and shake you to the core.

When something big happens, jets streak overhead with a different sound than the military jets at home. These guys are in a hurry. At times, distant explosions are followed by machine-gun fire, and then the helicopters bound for the hospital. Heading for meetings, while enjoying Baghdad's garbage and dust-scented air, a close explosion can divert your direction to a bunker, where you wait for the all-clear, or a second explosion. Regardless of the heat, you have to stay put until you are told otherwise.

The other day, while talking on the phone with my wife, I hear a particularly close and loud explosion. The next day I read that a bus of people on their way to work were incinerated. When you hear a bomb, you know innocent lives are changed forever.

Our next day of *How to Build a Court* comes with a warning about new workers recently recruited from Sadr City. They also can't be trusted, but are good workers. Gee, thanks. The Iraqis aren't the only problem in the court. The courtroom is the newest photo opportunity for soldiers and civilians. People go up and sit at the judges' bench, holding the gavel, and making faces. This is forbidden and requires frequent action by U.S. Marshals and RCLO staff.

The fear, one ultimately realized, is that these pictures will end up on the Internet. I have enough stateside experience in courtrooms to know you don't goof around the judge's bench—at least while someone is looking.

Enough work for the day, so we take a road trip over to one of Saddam's sons' palaces. Named the "Pleasure Palace," it's not as big as one of Dad's places, but it still features lakes and ornate architecture. Our smart bombs have provided an open, airy feel to one of its sides, and created a skylight where a dome used to be. Supposedly, offspring Uday would cruise Baghdad, drag a woman off the street, bring her here to rape and torture, and then feed her to the lake's crocodiles. This would happen to women that accepted his flirtations. Also to women who didn't. It didn't matter to him.

This is also the location of three massive Saddam heads wearing a Babylonian warrior helmet. They used to adorn the top of the Republican Palace, but were removed by U.S. forces and placed in a motor-pool parking lot. Surrounded by tanks, one of the heads sports the wishful graffiti Hooters. We are within spitting distance of the Red Zone, so we keep moving.

A vendor has set up a shop nearby and features the best item I see the entire trip, one that I will forever regret not buying. It is a dancing Saddam doll, about eighteen inches tall. It comes with several outfits, carrying grenades, daggers and a walkie-talkie, and when turned on, it dances to "Hippy Hippy Shake." Dang, it is only twenty bucks, but I am too intimidated to get one. By the time I have my nerve they are all gone. Exploitive commercialization makes the whole invasion thing worthwhile.

We have to clean our work area every day of the talcum powder-like dust that gives Baghdad air its character. We quickly figure out that everything needs to be covered at night after seeing all the rat tracks and droppings on our equipment. Above us, in the open ceiling, pigeons walk through the ventilation ducts.

One morning we discover a worker has used our room to relieve his bowels. I can't say as I blame him, as the available restrooms are inconvenient, disgusting, and in a constant state of overflow. The only bathroom semi-working in the building is adjacent to the media room. Unfortunately, the media room has a sunken floor; so when the toilets overflow a large cesspool is created. How we haven't contracted cholera these first few weeks is a minor miracle.

Two Iraqi construction workers, Achem and Mohammed, are assigned to assist us. Neither speaks much English, so communication is done with translators and hand signals. Whatever needs doing, they do it. Those two are great guys that work really hard, crawling between the floors and running cable. I try my best at Arabic, and they appreciate the effort. Achem tells me his wife cries when he leaves for work, thinking he might be on television. After the televised October hearing, a couple of defense lawyers and a guard were killed. I promise to keep him off the air. Who can and cannot be shown will be dictated to us later.

Like so many Iraqi workers in the Green Zone, these two will not divulge their jobs to outside people, and they take long, indirect routes back home to the Red Zone.

The start of the trial is drawing near and there is still a lot of work to do. One day as we enter the court grounds, the courthouse guards have their weapons drawn on four ratty-looking workers. For the most part the Iraqi workers are decent, though others are scavengers, and that includes the police. Since there are basically no locks on the building, security will take anything that can be carried out at night. There are numerous incidents of just-installed equipment, and tools missing when we arrive in the morning. We perform a daily inventory, just to see how far we are set back every day.

We are not immune from temptation either. We have the good fortune of "storing" some misplaced leather chairs and a couch from the defense attorneys' office. These come in handy for guests, court delays, and the occasional nap. We are asked once in a while where the furniture came from, and we just say we've always had it.

It is a war zone, and we are in survival mode.

Every morning is somewhat of a do-over from the day before. Different court personnel will demand a video feed, because so-and-so has one; so additional cable has to be run several floors. We leave at night after audio and video cables are precisely cut and placed with microphones and monitors, only to discover an entire area of the court moved two feet by morning, with the cables stretched like tripwires.

Where Saddam is going to sit becomes an issue near and dear to me. The robotic cameras we are using need to be mounted permanently, and his final location is crucial. While some of the camera mounts can be affixed to plastered walls, the frontal shot is going into marble. In an American court, that just won't happen; in Iraq, it's not a problem. The Iraqi workers drill multiple holes into the marble. I then climb up a 20-foot ladder, hold a mount in one hand, while applying bolts with the other. Then repeat the process with a heavy camera. More than once these pieces of irreplaceable gear nearly suffer a long drop to the marble floor. I discover the ladder doesn't really hold on the slick floor surface, and one time it slides a couple of feet, with me on the top.

It is one of my scariest moments in Iraq: a sliding ladder, twenty feet up, holding a camera, with nothing but a marble wall to grab. Thankfully, a member of our crew hears my scream and rushes to my aid.

Another issue facing camera positions is being able to see and avoid people. Certain attorneys and the head judge will allow their faces to be shown. Others choose the reasonable decision of remaining anonymous. As mentioned earlier, this could very well be a life-or-death decision. The Iraqi guards are not to be shown out of concern for their safety. Additionally, some witnesses cannot be shown. To meet these requirements, we are forced to break a cardinal rule, by "crossing the line." That means that cameras are placed at more than a ninety-degree angle from each other—in effect, encircling the courtroom.

Upstairs in our sweat shop of a control room, soldering fills the air with acrid smoke. The unlucky few who can solder connections have burnt and blistered fingers from days upon days of building cables. All the wires from throughout the building have to originate from, or return to our room; including microphones and video monitors for all attorneys, judges, witnesses, and defendants. A microwave dish stationed on the roof of the court building beams the signal across the Green Zone to the press uplink area located at the convention center.

The wiring at the convention center is a treat in itself. For security purposes, all media uplink facilities are to be away from the courthouse. A room is designated for potential press conferences, even though anybody connected to the trial is miles away. When we first start scouting the area, we are led through the living quarters of Iraqi security guards. I can sense nothing makes them happier than to have a bunch of Americans trudging through. As the night shift tries to sleep, others are squatting on the floor around hot plates, cooking repulsive stews. The guards are not hospitable, so I'm not concerned about being invited to join them. We are escorted up to the roof to find a suitable location for the receiving microwave dish. It needs to be protected from the weather and being shot at. I can empathize.

Before we approach the roof area, we have to get clearance from American snipers on the roof of the Al Rasheed across the street. Things are dicey enough without friendly fire. While installing the equipment, we just keep moving and crouching; yet trying to draw as little attention as possible. From where I stand I can heave a rock into the Red Zone. All of us make a pretty easy target, since we are identifiable as non-locals; perhaps that big U.S. flag I am waving is a bad idea.

In any event, just as the cables are strung and secured, the dish in place, and initial calibration complete, an explosion goes off a few hundred yards from us on the other side of the wall. The American Al Rasheed snipers quickly respond and shots ring out. Our crew looks at each other, "Okay, that about does it for being up here, time to go."

While working with the Iraqis or during some of our breaks, I am curious about their perceptions and experiences. They are usually glad to oblige, and of course, the story revolves around Saddam. While lamenting the current living conditions, they are hopeful that improvements will be coming. Under Saddam there was a consistency; life was tolerable. Random violence did not exist, and they had a social life. People knew what to expect and they acted accordingly to stay under the radar.

There was security in knowing the boundaries under Saddam's rule. Now, the rules have been replaced with chaos and fear.

A constant story in the news is the sporadic power outages and water shortages in Baghdad. Public works were already in a crumbling state, but Saddam would funnel most of the resources to beautify Baghdad. He would then reward or punish other areas with power and water as he saw fit. Places like his hometown of Tikrit never had shortages. Now the strained grid is shared with the rest of the country.

The deBa'athification removed most of the public works force, so many departments were left to novices or relatives of the new government. Those who had experience are now usually restricted from government work. Government stipends for food ended, and already scarce jobs are further strained by an out-of-work army—an army of angry, frustrated men with access to large stores of hidden weapons and ammunition.

Anyone connected to the Ba'ath party, be it teachers, engineers, or doctors, is labeled and discarded. All Ba'athists aren't evil and corrupt; belonging just enabled them to survive in Saddam's world. The removal of so many middle-class, hardworking Iraqis, leaving them without options can only spark resentment. Cleric Muqtada al Sadr created a public relations coup by providing money, fresh water, and food. We hear stories of Iraqis being paid fifty dollars by the insurgents to plant roadside bombs. Even if such people don't agree with the insurgency, it is a huge sum in this economy. These desperate people need basic necessities, and will rally around whoever gives it to them.

Unfortunately, the coalition seems to focus more on big rebuilding contracts and not the average Iraqi. Of course, there is a huge number of downright criminal, violent, sadistic Saddam loyalists wandering the streets as well. Their meal ticket has ended and now they fear retribution from the new Shi'a regime. It is no small task for our military to operate within the peacekeeping and nation-building role they've been handed.

After several long workdays, we reach Thanksgiving. Dinner at the DFAC is hilarious. The staff has dressed up mannequins as pilgrims and Indians, and built a huge Mayflower model. Most of the food workers are Indonesian, so they must think Americans are nuts. Once again, the menu is an incredible spread with roasted turkey, prime rib, and every heart-clogging side dish imaginable. While chatting with the head chef, he tells me the dinner includes 3,000 pounds of turkey.

It is great to see our soldiers getting such special treatment. Many of them don't know when they will be home for a holiday. Or for that matter, whether they'll even get home.

Our set-up is nearly complete. The cameras are mounted and working; the control room area is good to go. We're down to dressing up cables. That is, until we come in one morning to find a NBC/Reuters engineer (immediately nicknamed "Sparky") has plugged his unauthorized transmitter into our power source, reversing the current and burning up two robotic camera motors. Besides almost electrocuting our engineer, this adds seven hours of work to our day, so we leave at midnight. The next day is not much better. Since we are on schedule, and seem to get jobs done, our crew chief is getting more other people's problems dumped on him. So as the other teams throw up their hands in surrender, we pull long days.

Since we are ahead of the rest of the crews, and our equipment is installed, one would think the others could build around us. Nope. We just keep installing and uninstalling. It is quicker than having others rethink their process, and easier than arguing. Then during the final dress rehearsal, the building's power source, an immense generator, dies. Until the problem is resolved, everyone stays. The RCLO procurement officer scrambles to find a replacement generator and get it delivered.

Ironically, after using up all the threats and name-dropping he can use in normal supply channels, the temperamental generator starts as quickly as it stopped. Disaster averted. Besides, it is officially crunch time.

Tomorrow, the trial of Saddam Hussein begins.

Chapter 4

The Al Dujail Trial

There is a great deal of criticism concerning the order of the trials. Al Dujail is a lesser-known offense, and not as media-friendly as the Anfal case that is to follow. The Anfal (Spoils of War) case involves the gassing of Kurdish villages, and the mass murder of tens of thousands. The media wants a dramatic opening to the proceedings, with lots of footage of dead Kurdish children; instead, there are incriminating documents, and pictures of destroyed orchards. Perhaps the Anfal trial would capture the attention of a worldwide audience, but to Iraqis, Dujail is a typical atrocity with which they are all too familiar.

Background: In 1982 Saddam toured to gain support for war with Iran. Dujail was a small, productive town of date palms and orchards thirty-some miles outside Baghdad. As Saddam's caravan was leaving town, members of the Dawa party, hidden in the groves, attacked it. The rebels were angered over Saddam's treatment and assassinations of Shi'ites. Saddam escaped uninjured, but wanted to make an example of those who would defy him. Members of the secret police, headed by Saddam's half-brother Barzan, local tribal elders, and officials, conspired to effectively destroy the town and its population. More than 1,500 people, including entire families, were taken into custody and transferred to camps. One hundred and forty-three men and boys would go to prison, and face the Revolutionary Court. They were condemned to death, most without trials. To punish what was left of

Dujail, the palms and orchards were destroyed, crushing the town's economy.

It is essential to be on time on the first day of the trial. But I'm an idiot and missed the bus. Fortunately, I find some of the RCLO heading over in their Suburban, so I hitch a ride; otherwise, I am screwed. There is no walking to work in this neighborhood.

The Abrams tank is parked out in the road again and the entrance is full of Iraqi soldiers looking tense. I always wonder: If something happens, will they defend us, shoot us, or just run? Once past the road checkpoint, we come up on a little building with an X-ray machine and a new electromagnetic scanner called the "Scout." These are the units that have created controversy in airports over their invasive images. My take: If somebody thinks a thermal-type image is sexual, they have a real problem. Outside the courthouse is a full contingent of heavily armed U.S. soldiers and various transports; it looks like Saddam's escort is here. Saddam has the Army code name "Number One." I then go through more security checks in the building, up the stairs, and finally past the bored Iraqi guard outside our control room.

Waiting there is a full complement of guests for the trial: Commander of Multinational Force Iraq General George Casey, Jr., members of the RCLO, U.S. Marshals, interpreters, and Judge Ra'id, the investigative judge who first confronted Saddam with criminal charges months earlier. During that hastily convened arraignment, Judge Ra'id Juhi Hamadi al-Sa'iedi faced down the deposed dictator. As a matter of formality, the defendant was asked to identify himself.

When Saddam declared himself as "the president of Iraq," Judge Ra'id flatly countered, *"Former* president of Iraq." A young, tall, strong, handsome man with piercing eyes, Judge Ra'id also issued a murder indictment against cleric Muqtada al-Sadr. To indict al-Sadr, one of the country's most dangerous critics, and then stare across a table from Saddam and lay out the case that Ra'id helped assemble, I say Ra'id is all M-A-N.

After dusting off our equipment, brushing aside the rat droppings, and powering everything up, we get the final briefing of how things are going to proceed. I am seated at the control switcher, and next to me are two robotic-camera operators. In front of us is a large monitor filled with images from our seven cameras, and the evidence feed; that is, unless we are playing *Grand Theft Auto* during a break.

Seated to my side is a U.S. Marshal, who will ensure we do not show forbidden people. He has direct communication with ISOC, who will make final determinations about televised content. We are given a seating chart, identifying those who can be televised: two prosecutors, four defense attorneys, the head judge, certain witnesses, and the defendants. The chart has all names spelled phonetically and isn't close to being correct. These seating charts are carefully guarded, since they contain names and pictures of the entire court personnel. In the wrong hands, the list can be a diagram for assassination.

The audio mixing board is directly behind me, where all microphones will be monitored and fed to the media. Considering Iraqis all like to talk at the same time, our audio guy is going to have his hands full. The rear table contains engineering and the program delay. An RCLO staffer and two Iraqi attorneys will monitor from that position. Judge Ra'id is there to observe his handiwork. Engineering will watch the televised feed and make sure it is going out to the microwave site, and being received at the convention center. Initially, the program delay is something few people outside the court know about.

The purpose of the thirty-minute delay is not to mislead the public, but to provide protection in the event a person or name is recorded, and will place that person in danger. Our delay allows an editor to insert a few seconds of a still frame of the Iraqi flag, with a graphic explaining the interruption. The insert is also used when the judge indicates to cut the broadcast feed, and for the curtains to be drawn.

This measure is only when the judge loses control of the proceedings. Needless to say, we will get pretty good at it. Since the proceedings are fed directly to the pressroom, the media are well aware of the broadcast delay. I am surprised they don't complain about the trial being manipulated or something like that. The reporters must find it useful, since they will often watch particularly feisty moments again, before filing their reports.

As we near the start of court, American soldiers with bomb-sniffing dogs search each room of the court. During the search of our area I go down to the courtroom for a walk around with my marshal; because once the court is security checked there is no admittance.

Standing behind the judges' bench, the marshal asks "Are you nervous? This is huge." Actually, I'm not. I have done so many trials before, and I know we have a professional crew; I am more excited than anxious.

Heck, most of us have just worked more days in a row than typical freelancers. This is great.

Looking at where Saddam will be sitting in a few moments is so odd. We have been around it, sat in it, joked about it; but now the guy who ordered the murder of thousands, started wars, and captured the world's attention will be right there in that black leather chair. I toy with putting some gum on his seat, but chicken out.

It is time to assume our positions, so the marshal and I head back upstairs. In heavy anticipation, with drinks and snacks nearby, we sit at our controls waiting for the announcement that court is beginning. In a telling moment of what is to come, we are informed the trial will be delayed for two hours to allow the defense time to talk to their clients. Are you kidding? They pull that defense tactic here too? Like the trial opening is a big surprise. Oh well, maybe transporting the defense attorneys to the IZ is the cause. It does give us time to reflect on just what is happening.

This is history, and not only are we witnessing it, we are participating.

Finally, one by one, the defendants are led in and directed to their seats. Each wears traditional Arabic clothing: a dishdasha robe and kaffiyeh headscarf. Iraqi guards stay close to the prisoners, so we really cannot show the entry, out of concern for the guards' faces. Once a defendant is seated, we quickly grab a close-up. The two rows of defense attorneys are already seated, as are the three prosecutors and their team. The judges have not yet entered. There is now confusion about which defense attorneys we can show, so we stay off them, and the prosecutors are huddled, so we cannot show them either. The defendants sit stoically, some in silent prayer. This is not great television.

Finally, Saddam is led in from the holding room, near the rear of court. He walks slowly and defiantly. Wearing a dark suit and open white shirt, his beard closely cropped and hair combed; Saddam looks more dignified than he did at his famous moment of capture. He surveys the courtroom as he is escorted to his seat in the front section of the defendants' pen. His co-defendants rise as he passes. Saddam is carrying a green Qur'an with gold embellishments that looks as if it has been damaged or burnt. The guards close the section gate and hold their posts next to their former president.

Saddam acknowledges Awad Hamad al-Bandar, seated next to him. The former head judge of the Revolutionary Court, Awad is charged with illegally sentencing one hundred and forty-three Iraqis to death without trials. Throughout the trial, he and Saddam will frequently comment to each other, and compete for the "Best Stink Eye to the Judge" prize.

From the judges' bench to the left, are the defense tables, two rows accommodating twelve attorneys. To the extreme left is an enclosed witness box with curtains, not visible to the defense. To the judges' right is the prosecution, with three main attorneys, and three support staff. In front of the judges are scribes writing down the proceedings. At off-center right is the witness stand, a few feet from the defendants' pen.

A highly caffeinated bailiff enters from the rear and quickly crosses the courtroom. He slaps the judges' door three times, and shouts a bunch of stuff in Arabic, something about "Makima." I think, "Oh crap, the whole trial is going to be like this."

Despite having a feed from the translator, the translation is not in real time and often nonexistent. Fortunately, one of the English-speaking guest Iraqi attorneys positions himself right behind me, next to the marshal, so I can ask for immediate dialogue help. As the judges enter, the defendants remain seated, despite all the attorneys and court staff standing. Head Judge Rizgar's face reflects his displeasure with this initial slight.

Judge Rizgar Mohammed Amin, a tall thin Kurdish man with gray hair and kindly face, will be the only person on the bench that we can show. He opens with a brief announcement of condolence to the defense for the murders of two of their counsel following the October hearing. After this gracious gesture, the judge is rewarded with a barrage from Saddam and the defense attorneys.

Saddam has his hand up first, so he begins his list of complaints. He doesn't like having to wear handcuffs. (That's a good one, big guy). Next, from his cell in the basement, he has to walk up five flights of stairs because the holding room's elevator broke. (Funny, it worked for all the other defendants, until it was Saddam's turn). Then he whines about not having a pen and paper. With that final injustice, the judge shows mercy and orders Saddam be given writing utensils. Saddam will later try to pocket the pen, but it is removed before returning to his cell.

Let's identify the rest of our contestants.

Seated left, in the front row, next to Awad, is Dujail Ba'ath party official Mohammed Azawi Ali el-

Marsoumi, who reminds me of Boris Karloff in a kaffiyeh. So old and frail, he needs assistance to get in and out of court every day. Throughout the day, his mouth will be open, head tilted back and eyes closed; we keep thinking he's dead. His being in the front is an error, and he will be moved to the back, away from the misbehaving children, Awad and Saddam.

In the rear row is Ali Dayah Ali, a lowly Ba'ath Party member, and son of the former mayor of Dujail. He is afflicted with wicked facial moles. Next to him is the singular "bad boy," Saddam's half brother Barzan Ibrihim al-Hassan al-Tikriti. Barzan always looks on the edge of going ballistic, a good qualifier for his job as head of Saddam's secret police.

The middle row left has Taha Yassin Ramadan, the mousy former vice president who will invariably pick his nose when I take a close-up of him. In the middle is Abdullah Kasim Ruwayyid, the stately tribal leader. To the right is his deadpan son, Mizhir Abdallah Kasim Ruwayyid al Mashari.

With a cast this unfamiliar, and the names way too long to pronounce for calling camera shots, giving nicknames is our only recourse. Ali became "Moley;" Barzan is just Barzan; Taha becomes the "Picker" or Taha; Abdullah is the "Sheik;" Mizhir is too boring for a nickname, so he stays Mizhir; Mohammed becomes "Boris;" Awad is "Dr. Evil;" and the star defendant becomes "Mr. Giggles," or Saddam.

Awad, the former judge, has such a dark look in his eyes that he must have terrified defendants. To face a judge who is powerful, intelligent, and has no conscience, would not have given the prisoner much hope. Saddam earns his court nickname from his creepy little laugh, followed by the grimacing of his teeth. He finishes each laugh by showing his teeth and staring at his subject. From a floor up, we can feel a bit of the terror this man must have inflicted.

I've seen numerous sociopaths in court over the years, and Saddam rules supreme.

Of course, our name-calling is dependent on which guests are in the room observing. You can't very well shout "Moley" or "Dr. Evil" with General Casey in the room. As we learn the defendants' names and faces, we will mostly use the real names, until we get tired and punchy.

The defense team is then given their turn to berate the judge, and they do not disappoint. Seated in the first chair of the second row, is a familiar American face, Ramsey Clark. Yes, the former U.S. Attorney General is there to assist in the defense of Saddam Hussein. Clark has an infamous history of protecting the human rights of such notables as the Chicago Eight, 1993 World Trade Center bombing mastermind Sheikh Omar Abdel Rahman, U.S. embassy bombing suspects, the PLO, and former Serb leader- butcher Slobodan Milosevic. A staunch anti-war advocate and a consistent critic of U.S. global policy, Clark is choosing to represent the rights of a dictator responsible for mass graves, torture, and destruction.

Clark's tactic then, and now, will be to try the case in the press with numerous accusations in order to stir up public sentiment. The first defense comments are limited to what legality and authority the IHT has. The judge brushes aside the challenge, and says he will deal with it later.

But Judge Rizgar is curious about Clark. By what right is he here? Clark is not Iraqi, nor can he speak Arabic. Even though Clark has submitted briefs to the court, that does not mean he can address the court while in session. Clark clumsily fumbles with his translation headphones, and tries to speak. The judge will not have it, so the Arabic defense attorneys have to argue for him.

Clark keeps trying to talk, and is repeatedly told to be quiet. It is beautiful. Finally, the judge offers a resolution, as a courtesy, to allow Clark to sit at the table and observe. Like a scolded third-grader, Clark sits down and complies; his headphones still askew on his head.

After all the testosterone subsides, the trial starts. The lead prosecutor, Ja'far al-Moussawi begins by showing a poor-quality public relations video of Saddam touring Dujail. There is a lot of the usual stuff we have all seen, Saddam smiling and frightened citizens cowering. One telling scene is from a rooftop, with Saddam lording over the waving citizenry. The cameras inadvertently catch the perimeters of the crowd, where guards with pointed automatic weapons ensure exuberant joviality.

The next section of the video is difficult to distinguish as an interrogation, but that's how the prosecution describes it. It looks like every other Saddam video, with him standing around with a bunch of soldiers, and frightened civilians trying to save themselves.

Next is the deathbed deposition of a former Ba'athist, Waddah Ismai'il Khalil, who gave an insider's account of the atrocities at Dujail. Judge Rizgar reads the transcript. Just like in the United States, judges and attorneys in Iraq really know how to grab the trial spectator's attention. Viewers at home must be searching for their remotes. The point of the former intelligence officer's testimony is that Saddam's men knew that no more than twelve or so could have been involved in the assassination attempt on Saddam. Yet, hundreds were rounded up and shipped to camps, and the town's orchards were destroyed.

So, with a video and a read transcript, that concludes the evidence for the day. However, Barzan asks to address the court. In the most sincere terms, Saddam's half brother asks to delay the proceedings because he has cancer. He reminds the court that he sent a letter detailing his affliction. In an early show of authority, Judge Rizgar argues the timing and validity of the complaint; he has never received the letter, and instructs Barzan to get a doctor's note.

"Stop wasting the court's time," Rizgar says. (For heaven's sake, judge, don't you realize how long it takes to get a doctor's appointment in Baghdad?) In reality, these prisoners are all under the care of U.S. military doctors. They are getting their teeth cleaned, and every other potential malady corrected. Their complaints are purely for the television audience, and will later border on the ridiculous.

Finally, another defendant wants to speak with his son, and starts to cry. The defendants start by addressing the court politely, until they hear "No," and then proceed to start yelling, pointing, and insulting the court. The defendants who once held power over life and death, and were used to intimidating their way through situations, are now on the receiving end of justice. And boy, they don't like the feeling.

Court is adjourned for the day, and for the week. The next court day will not be until December 5. In what will become a habitual issue of credibility, the court often recesses for long periods without explanation. The frequent breaks give all of us, and undoubtedly the world audience, the impression the court is either intimidated, or unprepared.

A disturbing issue that never makes televised coverage is the behavior of the Iraqi guards in the courtroom. While we can never show them, the guards escort the defendants to and from the holding room, stand near the pen until the judge enters, and then move to the rear of the court during the session. The guards are unarmed and wearing generic khaki uniforms without emblems that look straight out of the Dickies catalogue.

During the frequent court breaks, the guards gather around Saddam and chat. We don't know what is being said, but it has an air of a king holding court with his subjects. Leaning on the pen railings, I wonder if these guards can be swayed to help their former president. The conversations seem light and friendly, a little too friendly for guard and defendant. Fortunately, not seen on camera or by the media is an armed U.S. Marshal in an out-of-sight corner.

Even though he is just one guy, I ask him how many people he can take out before additional help arrives. "Oh, maybe eight," he replies.

I feel better.

The televised coverage goes very well. We have few security fixes. As we leave the courthouse, an Iraqi national that works for the RCLO, pointing at us, shouts: "Those men ... they are going to save Iraq." Okay, I was feeling pretty good before, but I'm not above taking an exaggerated compliment. To make our egos soar, that comment was followed by the RCLO head liaison telling our crew chief, "I just got off the phone with DC 1 (President Bush). Because of what you did today, dictators are going to fall. The whole world was watching." We aren't able to wear our helmets back to the embassy because our heads are too inflated.

The next week gives us a chance to catch up with all the additional requests being made for new viewing areas, fixing existing press area feeds, and general maintenance. One of the additional feeds requested is in the basement where the holding cells are located. We have been down previously to install a monitor in the defendants' area. By the way, these monitors only show what is happening in court, so the gang gets to watch a soap opera of sorts. Heavy doors and thick glass separate the guards and prisoners, who are kept in cells. The dark barren cages have two beds and a toilet.

After Saddam's tirade in court, he is being moved to a single cell away from his playmates, and needs his own television. He won't be able to pass notes to his buddies, but Saddam is well within talking distance. Freshly decorated in a lovely battleship gray, the oil-based paint will likely gas the former president before the verdict does him in. I look around his cell, sit on his bed, and get the hang of being a fallen despot. The sensation of isolation is frightening. It is as close to standing on Boo Radley's porch as I am going to get.

A small elevator takes the defendants up to the holding room adjacent to the court. The holding room is still under construction, and like the rest of the courthouse bathrooms, the toilet isn't functioning. This means all those old defendants have to take a slow ride downstairs at the breaks to relieve their swollen prostates.

It may seem like a minor inconvenience, but the air is so dry our gaffer's tape won't stick to anything. Plus, the custodians use heavy oil on the wooden tables that make our microphone cables sag and slip. It will not do to have some attorney get his legs tangled up and fall in court. We place microphones and monitors in each section of the defendants' pen, the defense and prosecution tables and the judges' bench. The monitors enable us to feed evidence in close proximity, rather than relying on the big-screen television sitting in a corner that only the prosecution can see.

With thirty monitors and microphones, our cables are everywhere but must not be seen, or become an issue. It is a constant battle of taping and tucking, all so Saddam will not grab a cable and strangle someone.

Chapter 5

Okay, We Are Really Starting Now

December 5 comes along and the court plans an "early" 10 a.m. start. Finally, we will get down to the trial. Our crew has to be at the court by 6:30 a.m. to clear security before the bulk of the court staff arrives, or before the media can see us. It also gave us time to recheck our recheck of our rechecked equipment. We have all stuffed tons of food in our pockets so we have breakfast and snacks. We quickly learn to remove all uneaten food, since that only seems to encourage the rat-foraging at night.

In what will become a usual occurrence, we receive the early bad omen from ISOC detailing what kind of delay to expect for the day. Today's is a whopper. The entire defense is threatening to walk out on the trial to protest the legality of the court. However, ISOC gives us a bonus of two additional faces to televise, Judge Sa'aed Mousa Al Hammash, and Saddam defense attorney Khalil al-Dulaimi. However, as we are about to see, the drama in the court far over-shadows the actual proceedings, and only fuels the perception of a joke trial.

Finally at noon, the judges enter first to avoid another embarrassing slight from the defendants. The prisoners are then brought in, and in a quick bit of improvisation, the defendants remain standing until Saddam is seated. You can see the displeasure in Rizgar's face. This bit of game-playing will continue a few sessions until the powers that be learn to bring Saddam first, thereby removing the defendants' insult to the court.

To slam the brakes on an already sputtering trial, Judge Rizgar opens the day allowing the defense to argue their complaint concerning the legitimacy of the court. Attorney Najib Al Nu'aymi moves to the defense podium along with Ramsey Clark, and attorneys Khalil al-Dulaimi and Issam Al Ghazzawi. Clark again wears his ill-fitting translation headphones. The motion delivery is swift and professional, and seems to make partial sense.

Their argument is, under Iraqi law, a court is considered illegal if it is established under occupation. Point for the defense. Further, the defense says the court is not independent, and is being influenced by the government. Hardly. As we will find, this court is stubbornly independent, since no one from either government can motivate them to get in gear. And the final defense argument is the IHT was formed after Saddam was arrested, specifically to try him for genocide crimes he committed twenty years earlier. Though it is doubtful that Saddam's Iraqi regime had an existing human-rights tribunal standing by. Good arguments, but noticeably missing is the "My client is innocent" proclamation.

The judge neither denies or addresses the arguments, and simply moves to call the first witness. With that, Clark and all but four of the defense attorneys get up and walk out.

What if you hold a crimes-against-humanity trial and nobody stays? We find out the court, or someone, has a contingency plan. Behind closed doors is an array of court-appointed defense attorneys waiting for an opening. This group can fill in should there be a walkout, or more likely, an unexpected death of a defense attorney. But since it is lunchtime, cooler heads prevail and the court takes a break.

After a lengthy respite, the trial finally sees its first witness. The approaching witness steps up to a small platform and witness podium. On the podium rests a large Qur'an. Standing just a few feet from Saddam, the witness testifies about seeing mass arrests in Dujail.

I marvel at his bravery. Never would he, or any Iraqi dreamed of standing so close to Saddam, with his back turned to the former dictator, testifying against the brutality of the regime. With perhaps a little too much bravado, the witness allows his face and name to be televised.

We are stunned when the defendants are allowed to direct questions to the witness through the judge. The judge then rephrases the question, hears the answer, and then repeats the answer back to the defendants. A speedy trial is not in the cards. The defendants glare at the witness throughout his testimony, as he fingers Taha for the destruction of the orchards, and Barzan for the mass arrests of Dujail citizens. Saddam has the look of *Had this been another time and place, you would not dare speak these words*. Saddam's half brother Barzan is the most vocal, criticizing the testimony as nonsense, and made up for television. Barzan rises, begins in a gentle, pleading tone and builds to a climax filled with insults. Barzan provides endless commentary and entertainment until he is hanged a year later. The day mercifully ends at 7:30 p.m.

The next day, our first order of business is to prepare the witness booth. After the first witness had his name and face beamed around the world, the following witnesses prefer to testify from behind a curtain and have their names withheld. Though the curtain is open to the judges and prosecution views, none of the defendants can see their accusers. Some of our cameras are in a position to see the witnesses' faces, but we respect the court's order not to show them. The microphone in the witness booth is outfitted with a modifier to make witness voices unidentifiable.

Initially, the modifier works so well that nobody can understand what is being said. The voice sounds like a gargling Klingon. After complaints from the defendants and their attorneys, our audio technician dials back the distortion. Even so, the women witnesses still sound like men from Mars in a bad sci-fi movie.

A string of nameless witnesses, referred to as "A", "B", etc., proceed through their angry and emotional testimony. Tales of torture, separation of families, and imprisonment are the common thread. As the defendants asks their questions, and the judge relays the questions, Saddam tires of third-party intervention and objects. One of our Iraqi attorneys tells us that under law, the defendant is allowed to directly ask the witness questions. Saddam is the first to bring up this right under Iraqi law. But the IHT has made a change in the ability of the defendants to speak to the witnesses. The trial rules were modified to eliminate this right, and avoid any intimidation or political speeches from the defendants.

But after hearing Saddam's objection, the judges choose to ignore the IHT guidelines and grant the defendant's request to speak. This decision ensures that the trials won't be quick or efficient.

Saddam sits, listening to the testimony, using his Qur'an as a table to take notes. Saddam and Dr. Evil also cross their legs, showing the bottom of their shoes to the court. We are instructed by our handlers not to feature these disrespectful acts by Saddam, since it might cause unrest within the Iraqi viewing public. A quick note: Secretary Rumsfeld was condemned in the Middle East for a photograph of him with his legs crossed, revealing the soles of his shoes. There is even a mural painted in Baghdad of Rumsfeld's atrocity. Apparently, something so natural in our culture is the height of disrespect to Arabs.

There is however, no comment from the Arab world on the defendants' constant picking of noses and teeth.

After the last witness completes their testimony, Saddam asks to question the witness, and is given permission. Fresh from insulting the Qur'an, Saddam starts with a religious salutation that is followed by an inflammatory political diatribe. He lashes out at the U.S. and Zionists for wanting him to be executed. He says the trial insults Iraqis, and that citizens should rise up and fight.

Our handlers freak out as Saddam speaks to his faithful watching on semi-live television. That "call to arms" scares me too. I know we have lots of troops around, but what if the masses sitting in hookah bars watching the trial react and there is total anarchy? The daily mortars and rockets are already enough for my nerves. The Iraqi attorneys in our control room are excitedly apprehensive at the prospect of Saddam's words getting out. We are instructed to delete Saddam's remarks before they reach the airwaves. As much as I appreciate the safety aspect of the order, it also smacks of censorship. These early days will see any negative comment about the "Occupiers" deleted. As we progress through the trial, and a Saddam-inspired uprising fails to develop, these restrictions and fears will ease.

Saddam and his co-defendants continue to employ the strategy of grandstanding after compelling testimony. Saddam understands the media well, and knows it can be suckered into highlighting outbursts, and forgetting earlier testimony. An unhinged Saddam makes an easier and better news sound bite than witnesses that cannot be shown. As we watch news from around the world, Saddam's ploy is effective; the focus is on the drama created by the defendants, not the tragic testimony of a destroyed community.

Ultimately, within Saddam's political proclamation there is no question for the witness. He has not heard or cared one bit for the trauma these witnesses have endured. It is he, not them, that is suffering injustice. When the judge cuts Saddam off from further statements, the former dictator threatens to boycott the proceedings. And the judge mercifully ends the day. As we wait for transportation back to the embassy, it is as dark outside as when we arrived.

The next day begins as the day before, an early arrival and wait. The court's 10 a.m. start moves to 11, and drags to midday. We can't leave; besides, there's nowhere to go. However, we are given some good news: Lunch is arriving. As quickly as my gastronomic hopes and dreams seem realized, they evaporate in the dry desert air. A feast fit for a Bedouin of curried gray meat kabobs, literally dirty white rice, hummus, and bread arrives for our dining pleasure. Some brave souls on our crew energetically devour the mystery meat, and will pay dearly later. I can't stand to even look at it, let alone eat it, so I stick with healthier food sources like Doritos and Frosted Flakes.

As I wait for the curry stench to lift, the long waiting continues. We have no idea what is going on. The radios are silent from ISOC, which means what is happening is none of our business. That, or everybody left and forgot to tell us.

A lot of the start times depend on the logistics of moving the defendants from Camp Cropper, and getting the judges, defense counsel, and witnesses to the court safely. But time for prayers and tea also dictates schedules. The spectators, media, and court support staff will be ready to go, with our military on standby, and we get a call that the judges have broken for tea. That will spill over to prayer time, and need to be followed by lunch. Hence, a morning start might easily flow into the early afternoon that includes more prayer and tea.

I ascribe this to a cultural philosophy of: "What can be done today, can also be done tomorrow." An Iraqi friend explained: If a houseguest is very late, or does not arrive on the arranged day, the host adjusts, and is glad the guest even shows up. I guess Hawaii's "Hang Loose" attitude originated in Mesopotamia.

After a four-and-a-half-hour wait, Saddam and his attorneys enter to a closed session of court. The drapes are drawn across the public viewing windows, and the live television feed is off, so reporters have no idea anything is going on. Saddam is basically pouting and refusing to attend the day's session. Judge Rizgar says fine, and returns Saddam to his holding cell, with that brand-new television and video feed to it. Saddam can watch alone as the other defendants, namely his half-brother Barzon, grab the spotlight.

Barzon repeatedly interrupts witnesses during their testimony, either to intimidate or to dilute the narrative. The witnesses never seem frightened, and in fact are lucid and resolute. But their story will not lead the news; instead it is Barzon's antics, and Saddam's absence.

And so court adjourns for two weeks for the upcoming elections.

Chapter 6

The Birds and the Bombs

After weeks of long hours, little sleep, and frustration, we have a morning to relax. As a freelancer, I'm not used to working so many days in a row. I take a morning stroll around the palace grounds and experience a sense of wonderment as I pass the buzzing activity of Humvee convoys heading out to patrol and soldiers at the 50-caliber machine gun mounted on the roofs. I hear dialects and see uniforms from the various coalition forces: Dutch, Australian, South Korean, and British. I don't see any Georgians on the compound; they probably can't be trusted around women. Those guys are only seen manning exposed outposts directing traffic.

During the daylight the palace is beautiful and imposing. The massive Babylonian style structure next to a date grove along the banks of the Tigris must have presented an impressive and forbidding sight to the regular citizens across the river. Now, as the hub of the Green Zone, concrete blast walls surround the former palace. Manned guard towers survey the river, with orders to shoot to kill. Saddam would undoubtedly approve of the refinements. Considering the pollution level of the river, even crossing the Tigris should be considered a suicide mission. Insurgents will likely glow by the time they reach the opposing bank.

My appetite led me to the DFAC for an indulgent breakfast. Located across the entrance of the dining hall is a barrel encased in sandbags. This is where everyone with a weapon has to clear his or her gun before entering. As a civilian contractor, it might look cool to carry a sidearm, but having to check your weapon every time when entering a building seems a real pain. Once inside I have to watch my step walking around tables, since the soldiers lay their rifles at their feet. It takes a bit of coordination not to spill a tray of food, or kick a stack of automatic weapons on your way to a seat, but it is one of those things you end up doing naturally.

For me, every meal at the DFAC is a treat. Sure, I hear plenty of complaints about this and that; but these knuckleheads who are complaining don't appreciate where they are, or the fact many of our guys a short distance away are eating MREs (Meals Ready to Eat). Or better yet, ask an Iraqi what they had for their last meal. These spoiled "food critics" will probably be treating their girlfriends to the fine dining of Sizzler once they get home to Arkansas.

The DFAC is a large temporary building adjacent to Saddam's pool. Next to the pool is a pool house, an outside movie theater of white painted plywood, ping-pong tables, billiard tables, horseshoe pits, and an aviary. The aviary is my little sanctuary, filled with parakeets and lovebirds. Their happy chirping and endless activity can make me forget where I am. As I begin my day, this is where I sit and call my wife to say goodnight. An Iraqi national cares for the birds every day, cleaning and feeding his charges; likely, they have a better life than most people on the outside. On hot days the birds spread their wings, pant, and lean against frozen water bottles placed in the cage.

All day, every day, the peace is shattered by low-approaching Medevac Blackhawk helicopters, as well as "Little Bird" helicopters zipping over the compound heading toward the city. Then, of course, there is the routine sound of gunfire and bombs exploding across the river. For some reason, these explosions often occur when I talk to my wife.

"What was that? " she demands.

I can only say it is "something," since we aren't supposed to divulge that kind of information.

She figures out what "something" means by watching the next day's news.

We are on the phone when a suicide bomber boards a bus across the river, and kills 30 more than people going to work. I can tell it is bad from the sound and concussion, and my wife can hear it on the other side of the planet. But then noises can be harmless, like workers repairing a roof. My wife could hear the constant banging, and I had to walk over to the construction to convince her it was okay. Ironically, that building would later be hit by a mortar and kill an American civilian on her last day of work.

On the topic of explosions, but on a lighter side, along the riverbank near the Riverside housing complex stands the bomb unit. Periodically, they detonate recovered explosives. The loudspeakers across the complex start warning broadcasts hours before the event, counting down the final ten minutes. As two of our crew housed nearby watch television, they are apparently oblivious to the warning. When the loud repercussion rocks their trailer, and debris lands on their roof, the two bolt out outside in a panic expecting an invasion. Hopefully they had something on besides underwear.

One night, after I return to my trailer from the evening coffee-shop ritual, my roommate asks if I heard the commotion. I had heard casual gunfire on my way back, but thought nothing of it. Just then all hell breaks loose outside. The popping and cracking of guns pierce the air.

Being more curious than intelligent, we go outside to watch as the sky is lit with amber tracer bullets. It is very much like the scenes depicted during the air raids on CNN. Is it an attack? Are the insurgents making a move? Are our bombers coming in? My fascination with the sky show quickly ends when I hear bullets coming down on the trailer roofs around me. The *ting, ting* intensifies, so I make for cover.

It turns out Iraq has just won a soccer game over Syria in international competition and every Iraqi with a gun (meaning most) is celebrating.

I discovered a bullet had pierced my trailer roof directly over my bed the next time it rained. Not having a Home Depot nearby, I plugged the hole with some chewing gum, and heard it was still holding fast two years later.

Part of the Unites States' new rationale for invading Iraq is the introduction of democracy and open elections. Accompanying the eager anticipation of this grand experiment are threats from insurgents dedicated to creating havoc. The militants have warned Iraqis to stay away from the polls, or risk death. A day away from the elections, the Green Zone wakes to massive explosions that land very close to our compound. And of course, I am on the phone with my wife. Subsequent American media report the "eerie quiet" in Baghdad. Knowing better, our crew decides to forgo maintenance of our equipment and stay off the roads. Throughout the day we can hear loudspeakers and cheering from across the river that even the helicopters can't drown out.

Predictably, the media focuses on the rocket attack, and not the Iraqis expressing their newfound freedom.

The day of the election brings more morning explosions and a mandatory order to wear armor. Again, since no one knows how crazy the day might get, our crew opts to stay at the embassy near soldiers, except there aren't any. The compound is nearly void of military. I assume they are all out on patrol, because if there was a withdrawal, I'm going to be pissed. The day is quiet and uneventful, as far as explosions go.

Across the river, an impressive 70 percent voter turnout grabs the media's attention for the moment. Iraqi television shows huge voter lines snaking around the polls, putting to shame the apathy in our country. Elated Iraqis are shown in the media holding up their ink-stained fingers as a sign of independence.

After dinner I head over to the embassy coffee lounge, the Coffee Bean. There, ABC's Elizabeth Vargas is preparing to interview senators Lindsey Graham and Joe Biden. After, a group of about fifty soldiers gather around Senator Graham for photos and to shake his hand. Biden stands off from the joyous crowd, unappreciated, save for a few soldiers and civilians who want to check out his hair plugs. It is obvious the soldiers know who supports them back home.

Seeing our armed forces together, I am struck by the unique profile of Marines. Sure, their uniforms are different, but it is something else. Most regular soldiers look fit, but there are also a lot of reserves here, plucked from the comforts of being weekend warriors. Their waistlines expose years of neglect. The Marines, by contrast, are massive, pumped and primed. It is easy to spot them from a distance, with their V-cut torsos, straight backs, and firm walk. I know they are issued weapons, but they don't look like they need them.

With Iraq's cloud of tyranny lifted and the election a resounding success, we resume the never-ending dusting and cleaning of courthouse gear. Of course, there is a new ration of courthouse rumors. We hear Saddam won't make it to the summer, by his hand or someone else's. There is also talk the judges are trying to get the head judge to shut down the antics of the defendants. There is no talk of increasing the court's schedule to actually have trial days. After a few hours of removing the dirt and rat droppings blanketing the equipment, and using an entire bottle of hand sanitizer, we settle in to play *Grand Theft Auto* until it's time to go back to the embassy. War is hell.

There is still a watchful eye for the insurgents to make some statement after the election. Otherwise, their movement will seem defeated. If peaceful Iraqis stood up, they could root out the militants that are causing the deaths of so many innocents. But the pointless violence seems to be a sad part of the Arab culture, with Saddam and other regional leaders perfecting the art. While there are many regions where different sects live peacefully, grass-roots sectarian extremism and viciousness has persevered for centuries. For some of the disenfranchised, being a martyr or chopping off heads seems to be a strange heritage and solution.

The embassy address system announces the arrival of Vice President Cheney a short distance away, and advises us not to be concerned with the hovering

Apache helicopters. My concern is that he will come here and make us a target for mortars.

Chapter 7

Heigh Ho...

A month into this dysfunctional mess of a trial, and we are starting only our fifth day of proceedings. Security surrounding the court has changed drastically since we first arrived. An Abrams tank has returned to guard the street outside the court. The Iraqi guards at the entrance are much more suspicious and tense as they search our vehicle inside, under the hood, and underneath. Once inside the court complex, concrete barriers and blast walls block our normal path. We are directed toward a new route to the court that snakes through walls that lead to a new security shack. There is still an entrance that only allows military vehicles transporting the defendants through. Inside, we run our personal items through metal detectors and go through an added "Scout" backscatter X-ray machine.

Personal cameras are now confiscated until we leave for the day. So much for the souvenir travel photos. Thank goodness I made good use of the camera early on.

Along the road to the main gate outside the court, we are instructed to stay under the recently added awnings that cover the walkway. Iraqi manned guard towers now hover above the walkways. At the gate, we show our credentials again, and then proceed into the open space in front of the court. The surrounding cement walls have been modified with fencing and green fabric to shield the view of court entrants from the nearby apartment buildings.

We are told that residents in the building have been watching and might possibly call in an attack. To our right are the vehicles used to transfer the defendants, as well as armored personnel carriers and heavily armed Humvees. Everywhere around us are soldiers with guns at the ready.

Inside the courthouse, we go through another metal detector. We are then instructed to get an additional identification badge, issued by the tribunal that allows us access to where we need to go. Since we are the technical crew, it is basically a backstage pass to the building. One side of the identification is English, the other Arabic. It's interesting to see my name in Arabic, but they could have labeled me "Dog-Faced Man" and I wouldn't know.

From there, we begin the five-story climb up the uneven stairs. Each floor now has security, and we must show our badges to get to the next level. The court entrance on the fourth floor has its own "Scout" scanner and two guards. Even our floor has a guard outside the recently added door. Inside, we get a visit from the bomb dogs, which adds a bit of comfort and discomfort.

But, with all the changes to court security, we find nothing changes with court procedure.

We are informed there are six witnesses scheduled, with only the first permitted on camera. That means there will be a lot of shots of a curtained witness box with a garbled voice coming out of it. Then we hear there might be some written statement, from whom, we don't know. We wait and wait, until finally, at 11:30, the trial commences.

Saddam immediately takes control of the court again, claiming he and the other defendants have been tortured and beaten by his American guards. The prosecutor rises to confront Hussein, resulting in the usual shouting match. Saddam had complained earlier about not getting a pen and paper, having to walk stairs instead of taking an elevator to the court, and having to wear the same suit of clothes (remember, this is the guy found filthy and hiding in a hole).

But this accusation is more serious, and it also could be credible based on the embarrassing guard photos circulating from Abu Ghraib. The thing is, there are no noticeable marks on any defendants, and they look well fed, especially Barzon. Could U.S. Army soldiers act so stupidly as to abuse such a high-profile set of prisoners that appear on worldwide television? The judge reassures Saddam he will look into the matter and begins the testimony.

Saddam's inflammatory accusation leads the news of the day, and again overshadows the true tortured victims about to speak.

We are told the next day Saddam apologized to his American guards after court for the accusations against them. His act was all theater. In fact, these prisoners are receiving excellent care from the U.S. Army. Their cells are housed in a new facility with running water and air conditioning, which is much more habitable than the average Iraqi dwelling.

Everyone wants these guys to stay safe and healthy until they're executed.

The witnesses come and go with their recollections of the events surrounding Dujail. The defendants mock the witnesses throughout the day, and continue to postulate about their own injustices. The long day, with frequent lengthy interruptions, ends at 9 p.m.

The next day brings some initial excitement when a defense attorney carries a gun into court. I'm not sure where it was discovered, since the attorneys are picked up from an undisclosed location and escorted to the court. For some reason, a number of them insist on returning to their homes in the Red Zone at night, and not stay under protection in the Green Zone. It is a huge logistical nightmare for the court, and a dangerously stupid risk.

The Iraqi guards around the court are now divided between those looking bored with their new posts, and others wanting to shoot their AK-47s at someone. I feel neither secure nor comforted. My confidence in security is further diminished by the fact I inadvertently carry a six-inch bladed knife inside my bag to court. To show my trustworthy intentions, I report the incident to U.S. security. They borrow the knife and test-run it through security, again without the Iraqis spotting it.

It is returned to me at the end of the day, with thanks for my honesty. I am also told not to do it again.

Our first witness of the day was a young teenager at the time of Dujail event. He lost several family members in prison camps, and after returning from his own detention, found his home and future gone. The witness experienced firsthand Saddam's retaliation for the attempted assassination by ordering that the agriculture supporting the town be destroyed, orchards cut down, and fields bulldozed. Barzon chides the court for offering a witness that was so young at the time of the incident, and that a child's recollection could not be reliable.

Hey, Barzon, ever hear of Anne Frank?

Later in the day, when an adult female testifies about her children being forced into a camp, Saddam coldly replies he was only keeping the families together. This is the mindset of the defendants. Nothing is their fault; the loss of part or all of village's population means nothing compared to the retention of power. Anyone who questions the Hussein regime's absolute authority deserves to be punished.

Barzon has more important matters to discuss than listening to sad stories from farmers. As Barzon rises to address the court, Judge Rizgar wisely closes the session to the public, not allowing a forum for the defendant's incessant rambling. For two hours, Barzon argues the credibility of the proceedings, his incarceration, and his treatment. In all that time, Barzon presents three outrageous and pathetic complaints. One is that Saddam isn't "treated properly," and that Saddam is destitute, having not planned for retirement. The third complaint is the brand and number—six—cigarettes allotted daily in jail.

Barzon barks, "I have rights."

Witnesses had their lives ruined, their homes destroyed, and their families killed, but everyone should pity the poor half brothers. We are told by one of our observers, however, that the pudgy Barzon is fond of those gross kabobs served at lunch.

For some reason, the court recesses for the Christian holidays. Christmas will be followed by Ramadan, which means there will not be proceedings for over a month. We also hear there may be a change in head judge, since Judge Rizgar has about had it with criticism from all sides.

During the frequent breaks, workers have been busy preparing a secure room for our production equipment and us. For the past few days we have been breathing drywall and concrete dust. Considering Baghdad's air quality, not many of us can tell the difference. Instead of basically being in a hallway, our control room will feature air conditioning, lights, the couches we "borrowed," and bathrooms! No longer will mad dashes down flights of stairs be necessary.

Before the bathrooms are completed, it is tempting to use the open drain, but I decide otherwise. Unfortunately for some plumber, Iraqis working the night shift did not extend that courtesy. So when the pipe downstream was opened to complete the installation, surprise! As a poorly timed addition, locks are subsequently installed on the bathroom doors that only give us access.

To clear the area for the workers to finish our room, we are required to completely disassemble, clean and box our equipment, then wrap it in plastic. This is as much to protect from the dust and rats as from prying worker eyes. Our gear is the only of its type in Iraq, and likely the region, and not easily replaceable. Once everything is stacked, covered, and locked in an empty room, we depart for the holidays. Without court or equipment to clean, there is little need for us to return until things are ready.

Breaks like this are not welcome, since it makes time crawl, especially at Christmas.

Chapter 8

Happy Holidays

The MWR (Morale, Welfare and Recreation) has done an amazing job of bringing the holidays to the soldiers. Inside the embassy Christmas trees, fake presents, and cardboard fireplaces with stockings are tucked into corners around the Coffee Bean. Along the hallways and in the lounge, hundreds of handmade cards and letters from American schoolchildren wish the military happy holidays. I frequently stop and read the cards. They call our military "heroes," professing their hope for the soldiers' safe return, and thank them for their sacrifice. The negative clatter from activists back home is more than compensated for by these innocent, heartfelt wishes.

At poolside is a life-sized Santa and sleigh with reindeer. Lights are strung around the pool house, and holiday music is playing. It is an odd mixture of cultures when the Muslim call to prayer comes. Signs of the holidays are everywhere, from a group of Marines wearing Santa hats or antlers walking through the embassy singing "Rudolph" to an embassy fire truck driving around the compound with a Santa shouting "Merry Christmas." One soldier has a full Santa suit on, to complement his helmet, body armor and rifle. Even some Iraqis are wearing Santa hats. During a Christmas Eve MWR event by the pool, a melancholy crowd gathers around singing Christmas carols.

Like something out of an episode of *M*A*S*H*, low-flying Medevac helicopters momentarily drown out the joyful songs. In roughly another twenty minutes, more helicopters will come. Reality can smack you up the side the head around here. This is no winter wonderland.

The RCLO posts a message in our office from President Bush to us, the civilian workers in Iraq. Prefaced by a message to the military by Rumsfeld, Bush writes:

> When I read this, I couldn't help but reflect upon the sacrifice all of you are making this holiday season. Each and every one of you is a volunteer who has stepped forward to assume a role, which for the most part, will go unrecognized due to the nature of the mission.
>
> You are not in Iraq because you were deployed as part of your job… you stepped forward from a Justice Department and other agencies filled with good people… to do more. It is easy for our citizens to accept the spin of the media and complain about the war and what America is doing in Iraq and Afghanistan; and what we're not doing in the Darfur region and elsewhere, but not you… you've left family and loved ones to travel to a foreign land to promote the cause of justice and the rule of law, without which there will be no liberty or freedom. You … are part of the voice for hundreds of thousands who were brutalized and murdered.
>
> You have secured for yourself a place in history by the work you are doing. So, I want each of you to know that while I am here at home enjoying this joyous season… I will, at the same time, be cognizant and grateful for your willingness to sacrifice the comforts of home and family in support of the cause of freedom and justice.

That is a nice Christmas card.

The dining staff excels at Christmas. Massive cakes, gingerbread houses, and decorations greet everyone at the DFAC entrance. They even make reindeer and a Santa out of cake. While the final result looks rather mutant, the effort is well received. As usual, the food beats most of what people back home are getting. The average American likely doesn't have the choice of turkey, roast beef, ham, Cornish hens, and king crab when visiting Aunt Martha's for Christmas. After a meal like this, hungry insurgents can easily overtake the compound since we are too full to fight.

After Christmas dinner, the Fiji National Guard sings their traditional Christmas songs in the Coffee Bean. It is an intrusion on my space, but since it is the holidays, I let it go. The performance brings a standing ovation and beaming, proud faces to the singers. Many of us go up to thank them, shake their hands, and wish them a Merry Christmas. They are so moved by that simple gesture that many get teary-eyed.

I have such a goodwill-toward-men feeling that on my way back to my trailer, I stop at each security check gate and thank the Peruvian guards. A lot of people take these guys for granted, thinking internal security is a hassle. Not me. I like as many guys on our side to have as many guns as possible. My Spanish is weak at best, but trying to say "Feliz Navidad" makes a big impact. The guards smile and shake my hand, and wish me well. They probably make fun of the gringo after I leave. Regardless, I go to bed that night feeling like George Bailey in *It's a Wonderful Life*.

During this holiday break, and to combat the additional calorie intake, I decide to embark on an exercise program. The embassy compound houses a fine gym outfitted with all the equipment available at a gym at home. I've seen it often. I walk by it all the time on the way to eat. Covering the walls are flags from the various coalition partners. As the partners pull out, the flags remain. I'm guessing it's so we won't feel so alone. The guys working out in the gym are intimidating, pumping weights with physiques out of Greek mythology. It is demoralizing getting on a machine after a heavily tattooed Hercules, and setting the weight back to mere mortal standards. The soldiers' regulation t-shirts are stretched beyond known fabric tolerance levels.

I decide I want to look like that, but without the tattoos of tigers and women.

In my zeal to get fit fast, I load up the weight and immediately feel and hear a "pop" in my lower left back. I manage to shuffle home, skewed sideways as if walking between two parked cars, to my trailer and nurse the injury. Not to be deterred from dinner, I carefully make my way to the DFAC, catching my breath every few steps, and successfully negotiate the buffet table. As fate would have it, I swallow wrong and have to cough.

Suddenly, the room is spinning and I am dripping in sweat. I think I am going to pass out. To keep from making a humiliating scene, I grunt my way as fast as I can back to my trailer, trying not to break into tears around the soldiers. These guys are getting shot at, and I choke on a Pepsi. After a restless night from the pain, I waddle like a gimpy duck to the embassy clinic, conveniently located on the far side of the embassy. Admitting to the nature of my injury is as painful as the knotted muscle bulging from my back. The doctor gives me a shot, some anti-inflammatory pills, and sends me off with a sardonic warning that as we get older this kind of injury can happen. Thanks.

With little to do work-wise and my Mr. America training on hold, I focus on what news is reported back home, and contrast that with what we are told here. After working around news for a number of years, I am always struck by the "truths" that are actually reported. A striking case in point is the recent story on military recruitment. The American media correctly reports that new enlistments are down, calling it a rebuke of President Bush and a sure sign of failing support for the war. What Americans are not told is that re-enlistment among active military is up—in numbers that more than make up for the drop in new recruits. Over here we see photos and video of halls filled with soldiers retaking their oaths of service. One story, likely not told at home, is of a wounded soldier being sent to Germany to recuperate. He insists on being sworn in before he leaves Iraq so he can rejoin his unit, and finish the job. These soldiers would not do so without the full support of their families, and a belief in their mission.

As with any conflict, there are debates about the human and financial cost of war. While reading a biography of Lincoln, I noticed criticisms that could be pulled from today's headlines. Not that I am comparing George Bush to Abraham Lincoln, but the two wartime presidents share a common ground.

In the midst of the Civil War, the North had been suffering staggering casualties. It was not unusual to lose five to ten thousand soldiers a day in battle. Lincoln had come under heavy pressure from interest groups and the public. Congressional hearings about profiteering by contractors supplying war goods took place. The Democrats started openly criticizing the president about the length of the conflict and the mounting casualties.

To quote the book ("Abraham Lincoln," Benjamin P. Thomas, 1952. Alfred A. Knopf, 1994 Barnes & Noble, Inc.):

> *The Democratic Party came under the leadership of men of narrow vision or doubtful loyalty who were incapable of resisting the chance to reap political profit from the government's embarrassments." When Lincoln suspended habeas corpus (an act more restrictive than the Patriot Act), he reasoned that he had been entrusted to preserve the government with any power "not clearly illegal." Lincoln was accused by the Democrats of misleading the public about "the real purpose of the war."*
>
> *Democrats further declared that the enemy was unbeatable and urged for a negotiated peace, even though the South had never shown any such willingness. Lincoln, fretting about sagging enlistments and poor morale lamented, "...By getting a father, or brother, or friend, into a public meeting, and there working upon his feelings, till he is persuaded to write the soldier boy, that he is fighting in a bad cause, for a wicked administration of a contemptible government....*

Wars do last too long, they are not always popular, and the toll on lives terrible. Protests at home do nothing but demoralize our troops and their families, and uplift our enemies. A president has to make hard choices, and America is fortunate to have those willing to serve a cause that isn't always popular.

As the court shifts from a convenient recess to observe our Christmas and New Year, in the Muslim world Hajj comes next, followed by the Islamic New Year. There will be two New Year's observances this year due to a shortened Islamic calendar, based on the moon. The Hajj is where Muslims make their trek to Mecca, one of their Pillars of Faith. Unbelievably, some walk from neighboring countries. One of the prosecutors is making the journey, so chances are slim that there will be a surprise court day. Iraqis take their religion seriously. Around the embassy compound, Iraqi workers stop as the call to prayer blares from minarets across the river. Dropping rakes and mops, they head for the little prayer rugs they have stashed, sometimes settling for a small piece of cardboard.

It is a bit unsettling to be walking past an instant mosque, with all these guys prostrate in the dirt. But everyone shows respect and walks around them. When finished, they roll up their rugs and get back to work. And eventually, so must we.

Aside from burning trash and refinery fumes, love is in the air. Before the trial resumes, two members of our crew have decided to get married. Our female editor and one of the cameramen have been in a relationship for years, but are not permitted by military moral regulations to reside together over here. In the interest of domestic tranquility, and a heck of a story, the two approach the RCLO liaison. He arranges for a Christian minister from the Red Zone to come and preside over the ceremony in the courthouse. As far as we know, this is the only wedding to occur in Ba'ath Party headquarters.

Chapter 9

As The IHT (Iraqi High Tribunal) Turns

Once again we are shifting into long-day mode to be ready for the court's January 24 restart. Taking all of the equipment out of the boxes, we notice things got dirty even though they were bagged, boxed, and sealed. Our new room is close enough to completion to start moving in, meaning there's a lock on the door. In what was once an entry area with elevators, the Iraqis simply covered the doors with drywall and pronounced it done. They did hang a false ceiling with lights, but we can still hear pigeons moving about in the overhead air ducts. A large hole is left in the corner to enable our cables, and the vermin easy access.

It is there we discover the work crews have cut through our cables while building a wall. All of the cable originates from our room, and travels down to the basement holding cell area, the second floor to ISOC and the media room, the third-floor prosecution office, and the courtroom located on the fourth floor. There is no apology note, or anyone to yell at, when something like this happens. It just adds hours of needless work.

Santa granted my wish and the bathrooms are installed. Hopefully, the pipes are now connected, or somebody downstairs is going to get a shocker. Even though the odds of the toilets actually flushing rival winning big on a Las Vegas slot machine, it is worth the gamble. Our RCLO handler surprises us further with our own refrigerator, coffee maker, and microwave. I feel like Scarlett O'Hara: "I'll never be hungry again." Our abode becomes more civilized with a huge bag of

Starbucks coffee from my sister-in-law that I share with the crew.

Despite the complexity of reattaching hundreds of cables, our setup goes smoothly. We even set up a little lounge area with our furniture. From there we can comfortably watch satellite television while waiting during court delays, or take a nap, whichever comes first. We again disassemble the robotic camera motors and clean them, and re-bag them. During the holiday break, our microwave receiver located on top of the convention center across the Green Zone suffered some storm damage. We get to make the exciting trip back over to the roof area where we can be fully exposed to the Red Zone.

Every gunshot or car backfire sounds like your last moment. With the help of plastic zip ties, rope, and gaffer tape, we complete our task just as a Blackhawk circles overhead firing chaff flares, a clear indication to get off the roof and out of sight. In a few days, the television portion of the trial looks ready to go again. There's even an innovative red-light button for the judge to signal us to cut the transmission when the defendants act up. And a new graphic explaining the judge's order, so the media doesn't think there is some conspiracy. While it looks like we are finished, new problems present themselves.

It makes no sense to work quickly around here, because you are likely going to be told to change whatever was just completed. Take the courtroom. We had just spent hours under tables, on our hands and knees, recoiling, re-taping, and dressing all of our cables. The "new" head judge comes in, and wants the prosecution table backed away from the defendants' cage another five feet. Huh? All of our cables have been cut to length to minimize clutter, and while there is some slack, there's not five feet. Regardless of our disgust and frustration, there is no recourse but to re-wire. We are then told about the episodes of *As the IHT Turns* that we missed.

Judge Rizgar apparently had his feelings hurt by all the criticism, so he wanted to resign. Letters of support for the beleaguered judge from a group of attorneys failed to materialize as planned. One of the critics of Rizgar, a judge, often boasted about what he would do if he had the position. A panel took him at his word and said, "Tag, you're it." Then, Head Judge #2 panicked and said he didn't want the position, and he would resign if forced to take it. Then the other judges threatened to resign if Judge #2 resigned. Then #2 got really upset when he was told he would have to be on-camera for the proceedings. There were going to be meetings to try and get the judge to agree to show his face. Then accusations of #2 being a former Ba'ath Party member surfaced.

The issue quickly resolved itself by an IHT statute forbidding former party members from serving as a judge. With the defendant's frequent political speeches and restricted participant coverage, all we needed was a head judge who was camera-shy—and a Ba'ath buddy to Saddam.

We hope the powers that be have motivated the judges to get this trial moving. Everyone is tired of Saddam and Barzon ranting about their wants. The other defendants are fairly quiet, too busy picking their teeth or noses to make a fuss. It is a real problem trying to get reaction shots of these guys without someone sticking their fingers in someplace disgusting. We are told that the trial will start soon and keep going on a new, improved schedule. Not to mention more dramatic: The next batch of eyewitnesses saw Saddam and his gang performing the actual crimes. Plus, the prosecution will present a death warrant, signed by the defendants, ordering retribution for the citizens of Dujail.

I want this trial to move along so I can see the Anfal trial—the Kurdish massacre trial that is expected to be very emotional. The Kurds hate Saddam, and are not afraid of him, or the insurgents. At present, the Kurdish area in northern Iraq is fairly safe because the local Kurds removed the insurgents themselves. Even during Saddam's regime, Iraqi forces rarely entered the area. Only by dropping poison gas could Saddam intimidate the Kurds.

The next morning we head over to the court just to keep an eye on our equipment. I'm not sure there's much to do, but I can drink coffee, watch television, and go to the bathroom. Stopping at the DFAC for snacks, I'm enjoying my breakfast when Senator John Kerry comes in, followed by two young aides. Kerry orders an omelet, and tries to look comfortable. Since the soldiers are ignoring him, Kerry jokes around with the Filipino kitchen staff. The only people who will talk to him are the ones who have absolutely no idea who he is. It's funny to see a famous senator just walking around unescorted. When a general enters the dining hall, he is accompanied by armed, unsmiling soldiers who stand guard around his table.

Back in court, with the equipment ready, we fall back into standby mode. We are told to be ready for an unexpected hearing that never comes. We wait and wait until given the okay to go back to the embassy. Another wasted day at court. In the meantime, the insurgents are staying busy. Several car bombs have exploded across the river, and are easily felt on our side. There haven't been many incoming mortar rounds, however. That quiet is only disturbed by the political demonstrations across the Tigris. I swear several Iraqis must have been given bullhorns for Christmas. In exercising their newfound freedom, there are daily events that include lots of distorted shouting and cheers. At the conclusion of each rally, gunfire erupts in celebration. I'm not sure what the events are about; I just hope the organizers aren't calling for a rush of the embassy.

In talking with Iraqis working with us, they express fear of what may happen when the U.S. troops leave. Many think there will be a sectarian war between the Shi'ite and the Sunni. Like Christianity, there are many factions of Islam. It would be like the Baptists taking on the Catholics. The more optimistic guess that civil war and democracy will spread to other countries. Certainly, the Arabs have always had trouble uniting behind one cause or leader, so they continue with infighting. Their disdain for the United States' support of Israel's Palestine occupation is the only thing on which they can all agree.

Mind you, by restricting immigration and travel, Arabs aren't inviting angry and destitute Palestinians to their countries.

The Iraqis I meet are decent, friendly, and intelligent. They are engaging with broad warm smiles, and even funny. Outside the court is a guard station at a large inner gate. Ten or so guards watch as we enter in the morning, and leave at the end of the day. One young guard has piercing black pupils, surrounded by snow-white eyes that are emphasized by his olive skin. Each day I say hello in hopes he won't kill me. But I just get a blank stare that cloaks his intentions. After weeks of brash persistence, he has finally come around. Now he smiles, waves, and gives me language tips on how not to say something insulting in Arabic. I'm sure we'll be exchanging Hallmark cards when this thing is over.

The Iraqis have suffered abuse by their own government for so long. Then we force our way into their country and say this is the way it's going to be. They just don't know who to trust. I hope our forces can stay until the young Iraqi government and army can bear the load. I will hate to see an implosion that sucks down these kind people.

The Ramadan call to prayer starts at five in the morning, with a cleric who thinks it is open-mic night and continues for three hours. A large celebratory fire blooms from the city side of the Tigris, and sheep and goats throughout Iraq are likely shuddering from the inevitable sacrifice. The recharged bullhorns, honking car horns, and requisite gunfire into the sky all signal the holiday when the Shi'ite faithful lash themselves to account for their abandonment of Mohammed's son-in-law during a battle some 1,200 years ago.

Our helicopters are watching the festivities from a high altitude above the city. Several large explosions don't seem to dampen the party, and there are no sirens from our patrols over there, so it must be part of the fun. Since there is so much gunfire, and stray bullets falling our way, I decide to find a place with a roof.

Once inside the Coffee Bean, I can hear even louder rumbling. The palace is a massive building made of stone and marble, so you only hear the largest explosions behind its walls. Forgoing safety for the desire to eat, I cross the fifty yards to the DFAC. It's not an attack I hear, but a good old lightning storm worthy of Kansas. The rain is violent, and the windows inside the DFAC are lighting up like the Haunted Mansion. With long rolling thunder and flashing skies, the poor people of Baghdad would probably assume they are getting bombed again if not for the rain.

The storm silences the festivities across the river, and suppresses the dust and flies, but it hasn't stopped Karaoke Night by the pool. Huddling under an awning, the deluge and lightning continues as those with a need to sing in the rain grab the microphone stand/lightning rod and belt out their favorite tunes. Perhaps I am in a sugar daze from my chocolate sundae dessert, but these guys sound pretty good tonight. Maybe it's like singing in the shower; water makes people sound better.

Chapter 10

New Boss on the Bench

Will the new judge have the will to control the court? So far, the trial frustrates everyone, and appears as a comedy of incompetence. As the designated start time passes, ISOC tells us to avoid bad words, and not show the defendants standing as Saddam enters. There is a rumor that Judge Rizgar may show up, demand to be heard, and try to regain the bench. Rizgar is supposedly in town for eye surgery, which prompted me to joke of him appearing with an eye patch: "Arr, Saddam. Ye' be holdin' your tongue, or ye' be walkin' the plank."

Just forty minutes late, the judges enter. No Judge Rizgar. Then Saddam is brought in. This is significant because the judges entered the court last in previous days, but the defendants never rose in acknowledgement. The defendants did, however, rise as Saddam entered. To curb that defiant display today, the judges and Saddam are already seated as the gang is brought in. Well played by the judges. The defendants' seating positions are also changed with Dr. Evil moved up front, and Barzon delegated to the back. Defense attorneys also have new seating assignments, with Iraqis in the front row, and foreign lawyers in the back.

Missing is Ramsey Clark.

The new judge, Ra'ouf Abdul Rahman, looks like an angry Ben Kingsley. He begins the session with an explanation that Judge Rizgar has taken leave from the trial. Then, in a lecturing tone, and chip on his shoulder, Judge Ra'ouf states the trial will be ruled with more discipline, with no political speeches by defendants or attorneys. Any attorney questions must be presented through an Iraqi lawyer. That proclamation lasts about thirty seconds before being put to the test.

No matter what court or country, telling a defense attorney they can't talk at will goes against their DNA makeup. Asharq Al-Awsat Salih al-Armuti, a new attorney from Jordan, pops up and asks to address the court. Ra'ouf immediately instructs him to sit down and not interrupt the court. And for good measure, Ra'ouf pounds the gavel until the attorney gives up.

In Barzon logic, this makes for a perfect opportunity to challenge the judge on some of the court's injustices. He raises his hand asks to speak, and assures the judge it is important. In the control room, we sigh and know what's coming. After weeks away from trial, Barzon is fully recharged and energized. With the sincerity of a Baghdad magic carpet dealer, Barzon speaks softly and places his hand over his heart. However, Barzon's condescending pleading is abruptly stopped by Ra'ouf, who asks him what his medical condition has to do with the trial. The judge tells Barzon to speak with his attorneys and that the court will look into it.

"Now sit down!" snaps Ra'ouf. The fuse is lit and the Barzon bomb is set to explode.

Barzon decides that his best tactic is to bully and out-shout the judge. For the time being, the other defendants seem content to let Barzon take the heat. Our interpreters are straining to keep up with the exchange as the judge shouts, "Sit down and shut up" to the inconsolable defendant. Barzon again complains about not having proper cigarettes, the American occupation, and the error of him being on trial. Ra'ouf holds up his hand and motions for Barzon to sit.

Barzon then insults the court by calling it illegal, and "the daughter of a whore." In any country, to any judge, that seems like a phrase not likely to work to any defendant's advantage. Amidst the laughter in our room, we can't believe what we are hearing. Judge Ra'ouf takes control and tells the guards to remove Barzon. The prosecution sits amused, seeming to enjoy the show.

Unfortunately, we are unable to show any of the Iraqi guards, so we keep the cameras on the judge. What we can't show is the comical removal of Barzon as he wrestles with numerous guards. The guards are tugging at Barzon's arms and pulling in a polite manner reserved for the courtroom and the observing media in the gallery. Like a high school girl rejected at a cheerleader tryout, Barzon doesn't want to go. He kicks and twists as the swarm of guards drag him off to the holding cell. All the while, we can only show reactions of the judge and attorneys. A sure Emmy is denied. As the guards close the door to the holding room, Barzon's shouts become muffled, and then quickly drowned out by his ferocious half brother.

Not to be outdone, Saddam rises and begins shouting. "Down with America! Death to the traitor! Long live Iraq!" The dialogue is happening so fast, and we haven't been told to cut the televised feed, so everything is going out. Surely Saddam supporters are dancing in the streets. This display however, is not helping with the trial's credibility issues. Next, Taha and Dr. Evil get up to join Saddam in cursing the court. Ra'ouf's plan of discipline is working just swell.

Defense attorney Armuti rises again and joins the chorus. The judge asks Armuti how he can do this, as a man of the court. From my brief experience here, it seems to be standard practice "as a man of the court." The attorney waves his arms and shouts like a New Yorker hailing a cab. Armuti then assembles his papers and storms toward the exit. Saddam's lead attorney, Khalil al-Dulaimi, now gets up and tells the judge, if one attorney goes, they all go.

Ra'ouf responds, "If you go, you can't come back." This trial has degraded to the level of a children's playground. Since we can't show most of the attorneys, we are unable to show the chaotic exodus. They bottleneck at the door, ridiculous grown men wanting to hurl final insults before they leave.

Saddam is smiling. The trial has ground to a halt and appears to be a farce. The former leader now takes the concerned, rational approach and asks how the trial can continue without attorneys. Ra'ouf tells him that standby attorneys will conduct the defense. Saddam doesn't want those attorneys. Okay, I'm with Saddam on this one. If they are anything like our public defenders in the United States, Saddam is hearing the fat lady sing.

Not that there is a much doubt about the ultimate verdict. But perhaps I am being presumptuous.

Ironically, Saddam launches into a speech about injustice. Judge Ra'ouf tells him to sit down and be quiet. The "Lion of Iraq" does not accept that demand. "I was in control for thirty-five years, and you tell me to sit down?"

Ra'ouf responds, "I am in control now."

The former president is outraged. Saddam and Dr. Evil want to leave, but in a face-saving gesture, Ra'ouf orders them removed, in a "You can't leave, because I'm kicking you out" sort of way. Great, the main reason anyone would watch this trial is walking out the door. Saddam manages an obligatory shout of "Death to America ... Death to traitors!"

When the judge asks one of the remaining defendants about his lawyer, the meek defendant says, "Allah is my attorney." Without a beat, Ra'ouf responds, "Okay. But do you have local counsel?" Anywhere else, this would prompt laughter; but here, Allah is no joking matter. Replacement defense attorneys slowly make their way into court as if they just received the death penalty. We can't show them either. This is not television at its finest. Nobody of interest in court, witnesses we can't show, and a crime that occurred twenty years ago. The judge tells the remaining defendants that these attorneys will probably serve them better than their original representation.

Already looking worn down, Judge Ra'ouf asks for the first witness. Three witnesses testify they saw the defendants in Dujail. The witnesses name names and say they were subjected to torture. The remaining defendants scoff, and claim that one of the witnesses is just mad because her cell phone was taken. Apparently, the fact that four members of her family were tortured to death pales in comparison to losing a phone.

At this point, it is anticlimactic. The interesting defendants have left, the new defense asks no questions, and the court mercifully adjourns mid-afternoon.

The media has a field day with the day's events. The BBC reports that "Justice is on trial." Ramsey Clark, speaks from New York, "This is unfair." Despite the early chaos, the trial proceeded as best it could.

The judges reviewed the evidence prior to the trial, so there are no surprises in testimony. They can choose to hear as little, or as much, as they see fit. Attorneys are supposed to ask questions through the head judge. Defendants can question witnesses, but not make statements. If the defendant wants to make a statement, he may do so in writing, or in court at the trial's end. If the international community were not monitoring this trial, these defendants would have swung already. The Iraqi attorneys we work with see nothing wrong in the trial's progression. They don't care about the media reports, and find headlines like Iraqis Shocked to be humorous. In a country where beheading is an accepted form of justice, these seven days of trial are already considered "long."

Saddam in Arabic means, "One who confronts." His fan base has to be astonished to see him treated so. The Iraqi government wants to send the message that Saddam Hussein is no longer powerful and will never return. For over three decades Saddam inspired fear amongst his people, and showed defiance to the world. Now, he is before a judge that neither fears him nor tolerates his defiance.

We get word the bad boys expelled from court have settled down, and are meek in the back holding room. Taken downstairs to their holding cells, they get to watch the day's testimony on television, and scream insults at will through the bars. The court is demanding that the defendants ask permission to return. They will have time as the court awaits the Islamic New Year and the upcoming Ashura.

Chapter 11

Ashura

For all the infidels out there, the festival of Ashura commemorates the death of Huysayn ibn Ali, the grandson of the Prophet Mohammad. Islamic holidays seem to mark someone's death or suffering, prompting sacrifices. Ashura is most widely known for its dramatic parades of men and boys.

During a seventh-century battle in Karbala, young Huysayn was killed on the tenth day of the Islamic year. "Ashura," means tenth. With his forces surrounded by an invading army from Damascus, Huysayn and his troops fought bravely to defend the city and Islam. However, they were seriously outnumbered and eventually wiped out, and Karbala was sacked. In defeat, Huysayn and his men became martyrs for Islam. The story goes that several of Huysayn's surviving soldiers were so distraught over his demise and their failure to protect him that they began wailing and beating themselves about the head and chest. Thus began the charming tradition still found today within the Shi'a sect.

This practice was not allowed during the reign of Saddam Hussein, because it symbolized the battle against tyranny and oppression. Not to conclude that the entire Shi'a Islam sect is odd, but exuberant boys and men will chant, lashing their own backs and heads until bloodied, to show their faith. In extreme cases, men will cut themselves and their sons with swords to replicate Huysayn's last battle. There was an instance in which a father cut off the head of a son as an act of faith.

The Islamic media tries to show how the practice has scaled back from the chains and knives used in earlier times to just a symbolic flailing. As evidenced in pictures and video, many devotees still use chains with blades to punish themselves. Now, the Sunni (the sect of Saddam and the insurgents) think it was sad about Huysayn's death, but don't feel enough guilt to begin beating themselves.

Take note followers of the Old Testament! The festival also includes the time of the final resting of Noah's Ark, the birthday of Abraham, and prayers and fasting for the tribulations of Moses. The air is filled with calls to prayer from minarets and bullhorns. In this celebration, all sects participate, and a good time is had by all. Lately, however, these festivities have produced disastrous, explosive, deadly results for opposing sects gathering in large numbers.

Despite the hardships befallen on the people of Baghdad, they still find reason and courage to celebrate, with the sounds of horns honking, crowds cheering, and over-amplified shouting from loudspeakers echoing across the Tigris. And even though the natives are restless a short distance away, the lack of insurgent activity is a welcome respite for us.

For a more in depth look at the region's history, see the Afterward.

Chapter 12

Ba'athists Behaving Badly

By now the media has lambasted the trial as a circus. The big international reporters have left for other stories, and except for Iraq, much of the television viewing interest has waned. News of the trial slips further back into the newspapers and broadcasts. Even we are tired of the shenanigans and abrupt breaks. What appeared to be an historical event of bringing a tyrant to justice has been reduced to a seemingly disorganized mess. Lost in the courtroom antics is all the hard work by the IHT legal staff, and the pain and suffering of the witnesses. Saddam has controlled the trial through disruptions, and he has played on the inexperience of the court.

We are back in court for another day, a closed session with broadcast transmission only to the United States. Video feeds of the proceedings will be limited to the downstairs cells and to ISOC. The transfer of the defendants, one at a time, up the small elevator takes over an hour. That visibly upsets Judge Ra'ouf. Finally, there are only three lesser defendants present. Saddam, Barzon, and others are boycotting the proceedings. The defense attorneys want an apology from the judge, and the prosecution wants to force all defendants to appear. The judge decides to continue as is. Five witnesses testify behind the curtain. Testimony from a woman implicating Barzan with electrical torture fails to reach the Iraqi public.

The next day, all of the defendants receive the boycott memo and refuse to appear. We hear chatter over the security radio that Barzon is causing a stir in his holding cell. Undeterred, Judge Ra'ouf addresses the court, and explains his legal basis in continuing the trial without the defendants. The judge states that the defense attorneys and defendants are violating court rules by refusing to appear.

That may be so, but it makes for crappy television.

Continuing, two witnesses testify seeing torture, and the public defenders do an effective job in questioning their memory and facts. Without any of the defendants present, so what? Another lackluster day. Everyone is frustrated, so Judge Ra'ouf adjourns the trial for two weeks.

My time in Baghdad is growing short. I agreed to a limited assignment, taking me to the end of February. It has been a long three months. Since none of the original group has been kidnapped or killed, people are begging to come over and be part of the television crew. Everyone hears about the long court breaks, great food, and good pay. My replacement is excited. He can have it—I'm ready to go. There comes a time when the money isn't worth being away from home, or the frustration, the fear, and outright boredom.

I'm thinking the measured pace of twelve court days in three and a half months can become an inspiration to the legal community worldwide. The determination by these trial judges to preside over a fair and orderly hearing of facts will shine like a beacon to procrastinators everywhere. I am hoping, at least, my last court days will be interesting so I can leave with a semblance of pride.

Our next day in court is a command performance. We are given permission to show two witnesses, and the defendants are being forced to attend. As a bonus, Saddam is led into the court, shackled. To prevent Sunni riots in the streets, we refrain from showing the hardware. The other defendants file in quietly, taking their seats.

In the back row by the media viewing window is Barzon's chair. We wait patiently, and then Barzon enters. Obviously not prepared, or desiring to attend today's session, Barzon is dressed in his long underwear. The saggy, cream-colored long johns create a stark contrast for the vitriolic henchman. Our control room erupts in laughter as we try to remain focused on our jobs. Looking somewhat sheepish, Barzon takes his seat. Hard-line regime supporters viewing this spectacle had to be cringing at the pitiful display.

Sparked by his half brother's defiant fashion statement, Saddam stands and begins shouting, "Long live Iraq! Down with the traitors! Down with Bush!" Here we go again. Barzon now joins the chorus, directing his diatribe at the judge. Judge Ra'ouf orders the brothers to take their seats. Saddam wants to continue the argument, but Barzon chooses to sit, albeit on the floor.

Like an angry two-year-old, Barzon turns his back to the judge. Out of sight to the judge and most of the court, Barzon is tucked near his chair, as the other defendants pretend not to notice. By moving our center camera, usually reserved for the judge, and located directly above Barzon, we are able to tilt down and capture the full glory of a hissy fit. Thank goodness for multiple robotic cameras. This is a classic shot that will live forever. The judge tries to proceed as if nothing is out of the ordinary.

Judge Ra'ouf's strategy must be to bore the defendants into submission as he reads scores of witness complaint statements. He then calls a witness that was head of Saddam's office, and has an intimate knowledge of events. Barzon becomes interested and calmly retakes his chair. Prosecutor Ja'afar presents several documents with references to "executions" and "No mercy." The witness confirms the signatures at the bottom of the documents are in fact, Saddam Hussein's. The witness must now realize he has implicated his former boss, and tries to make a hasty retreat by refusing to answer any more questions.

Ever benevolent, Saddam praises the witness for the show of defiance. Ra'ouf dismisses the witness and court for the day. Barzon is free to finally get dressed.

Earlier in the day, a major news story had broken in the United States. Vice President Cheney had accidentally shot his hunting partner. A reporter prophetically told us, "Unless Saddam moons the judge, your story is dead." Well, Barzon in his underwear was pretty outrageous, so we made the news. Iraqi media and public opinion soundly trash Barzon for "looking like a baby in a crib."

The next morning we arrive at court to have our power transformer erupt in flames when it is turned on. Thank God it isn't the coffee maker. Our engineer has to frantically make new connections from the melted parts before showtime. Fortunately, we are on Iraqi time and urgency is not a recognized concept.

Around noon, the defendants enter the court shouting, "God is great" and so forth. Barzon must have been so comfortable the previous day that he decided to wear his long underwear again. Saddam tells the judge they have been on a hunger strike, but none of us are buying it. Chubby Barzon likes the food too much, and these guys are not used to sacrifice. Saddam again complains about being treated badly by the Americans.

Like before, this is theater for the benefit of the television audience. These defendants are looked after by American doctors, and protected by American soldiers. If the Iraqis had Saddam alone for a few minutes, this trial would be short one defendant. Judge Ra'ouf takes the complaint in stride, and can probably see food stains on Barzon's long underwear. The first witness is called.

Behind the curtain in the witness box, with voice electronically garbled, the witness takes his oath, and Barzon interrupts. As usual, Barzon starts in a respectful tone, but quickly accelerates to get as many words in as possible before he is told to be quiet. The outburst is mercifully brief; however, Barzon unwittingly implicates himself as being part of the Dujail "assassination investigation." Oops.

Prosecutor Ja'afar presents the day's three witnesses with signed documents, and elicits eyewitness accounts implicating Saddam, Vice President Taha, and Barzon. The witnesses, all former regime staff members, try to mitigate their own involvement by admitting they also signed the documents but didn't have their glasses at the time. Barzon's attorney complains the document signed by his client is a forgery, and requests that a handwriting expert examine the evidence.

Nice try, but Ra'ouf tells the attorney the court will look at it later. Yeah, like after the guilty verdict. Judge

Ra'ouf adjourns court for two weeks, meaning I have just witnessed my last day of the trial. Saddam is sixty-eight years old, and Iraqi law forbids executions for those seventy or older. There are numerous trials to go, so these delays are Saddam's friend.

I take a final bittersweet look around the control room we built from scratch. What started with dust, stacked cases, and rats, is now an air-conditioned, comfortable, working broadcast facility. I walk through the now-empty court, recalling the installation of the camera mounts, microphones, and all the cabling. Despite the numerous courtroom dramatics, events in this room were watched worldwide.

I take a final long look at Saddam's chair. A few minutes ago, one of the world's most infamous people was sitting right there. I make final stops at ISOC, and then over to the media room that was once flooded by backed-up toilets. As I exit the court, the military convoy that will transport the defendants is standing by.

Going through the heavy metal gate, I see my new guard friend. The scary glare is replaced with happy eyes. Now that I am practically Iraqi, I hold my hand to my chest and bid him, "Asallam Alaikum." Meaning "Peace be upon you." We shake hands and say farewell. I don't think he has any idea that I'm leaving, and I feel sad for his country.

Chapter 13

Final Days

While the violence in Iraq remains, it is now less common, but no less tragic. The indiscriminate bombing of marketplaces, crowded buses, and children going to school has no point but to create fear. Islamic clerics, fearful of losing their position and influence, keep silent, while the radical minority encourages violent protests against the "blasphemers."

With so many followers unemployed and uneducated, the impoverished and ignorant await their marching orders. The frustrated population refuses to blame their religion, or government for their oppression and alienation from the modern world.

With American flags to burn supplied by clerics, the protesters vent their anger toward the only place acceptable. In this honor society, men see nothing wrong in getting paid to dig a hole that will be used to plant a bomb. The act provides income and a sense of pride. If deaths occur, it is "God's will" or the "occupier's" fault, not theirs, or the insurgents'.

While it has been generally quiet around the embassy compound, I hear a Katyusha rocket go overhead as I walk to lunch. It must have been a dud, since there is no explosion. After my dining experience, three more rockets follow, hitting the perimeter and shaking my little trailer. Come on guys, wait a couple of days before I get the heck out of here. The Katyusha rockets are easily fired from a hidden location and notoriously inaccurate. There is no aiming involved, and the rockets are meant to kill or destroy indiscriminately. The attack awakens patrol convoys that head to the city with their sirens warning of their approach, and causes Apache helicopters to circle above the embassy a few hours.

The excitement is quite an introduction for my replacement, who arrives by helicopter a short distance from the embassy. I meet him in the grand foyer and give him a big hug: "Man, am I ever glad to see you."

I've had enough bombings and shaking, and am ready to go home. Just two more days and I go to Baghdad International Airport (BIAP) to fly to Amman, spend a night, then on to the blessed United States of America.

Next morning comes bad news of a Sunni attack on the Shi'ite holy site of Askariya in Samarra, about sixty-five miles from Baghdad. The brazen attack heavily damages the mosque's signature golden dome, exposing mud brick and tangled metal. The shrine houses two tombs of ninth-century imams, including the father of the "Hidden Imam," al-Mahdi, sacred to Shi'ites. Angry men across Iraq are looking for revenge, and many are flocking to join Shi'ite cleric Muqtada al-Sadr's Mahdi Army here in Baghdad. There are heated protests, there are killings, and it's punctuated by sporadic gunfire.

The people of Baghdad are afraid to go outside, and so am I. This is not a good thing to happen the day before I leave.

I have arranged to take a helicopter from the embassy to the airport's military staging area, and transfer to the main public terminal on the other side of the airfield to catch my flight. Though limited, the main terminal still has certain flights operating. I go to the MilAir (Military Air Transportation) office in the embassy to get status updates and make sure I'm not forgotten. They tell me that due to the unrest, all helicopters are currently only carrying soldiers. As I try to compose my spinning head, my only option is to ride the American convoy through city streets on the Rhino in the middle of the night. At this point, I need to do what it takes to make my flight in Jordan. I need to leave tonight, and have only hours to prepare.

I say my goodbyes to the RCLO staff and remaining crewmembers and head off to the staging area around 11 p.m. I am also required to wear my body armor and helmet during travel, so the last vision people have of me is me looking like a dork. There is no telling when the convoy will come, since it is on a varied schedule so the insurgents can't plan an attack. The waiting area is a small building, filled with people trying to read, sleep, or play cards. We line up our bags outside to load into a semi truck that will accompany the convoy. As we form a line to pass along and load bags, I make a comment about my heavy monster suitcase like it is someone else's.

At this point, I have no phone, no Internet, or any means to cry for help. All I have is a letter authorizing my travel, and a plane ticket to the civilized country of Jordan where there is a Starbucks. Around 2 a.m. the Rhinos arrive and we line up to get a good seat. I manage to get a window on the big armored bus. It's a long slow ride, so I may as well look for insurgents as we pass the darkened city.

I am in the lead Rhino and listen as the U.S. Marshal advises checkpoints of our approach, and talks on the radio with our military escort, the hidden U.S. patrols located throughout the route, and the helicopter escort above. While I take comfort in so many safeguards, there is always the possibility of an attack. The other passengers are lost in their own thoughts, or asleep. I keep a constant vigil out the tinted window.

This is only a seven-mile journey, but it is difficult to judge progress because our speed is so slow. We reach the halfway checkpoint, all concrete and sandbags flooded in an eerie amber glow. Just like the last time I passed through, it still looks like the loneliest place on earth. Thankfully, the checkpoint remains manned by U.S. soldiers. Our convoy pauses briefly then passes through, but then we slow just up the road at an overpass, the site of recent attacks. As the escort sprays the area with floodlights, the convoy continues.

At this point we are smack in the middle of Route Irish. Our procession continues its cautious advance until we reach the Camp Victory checkpoint. I am back on safe soil. Even in the dead of night, scores of tanks, supply trucks, and Humvees clog the roads as if it is holiday rush hour.

We arrive at the "Stables," the military version of a bus depot lounge for the fortunate leaving, and the poor souls just arriving. It's where my journey began three months ago. It hasn't changed since I was last here; in fact, I think some of the soldiers from three months ago are still waiting to be picked up. After tasting the coffee, I'm sure it's the same pot. From here at least I can call home to let my wife know my travel has started. It will be the last contact with a familiar voice until I reach Jordan. Now, I wait until 6 a.m. to ride over to the terminal. Some people sleep in nearby bunk areas, but I don't want to miss my ride, so I watch *Airplane* on my computer.

At first light, I climb into a crowded SUV with other disheveled contractors. At the terminal, I am let off at the curb with my bags, and the other passengers quickly disappear inside. Since the airport mostly caters to civilian contractors, there aren't many people around. As I make my way inside, I start to hear things from a gathering of English-speaking passengers I don't want to hear. All flights are canceled until tomorrow, maybe. The Iraqi agent announces the delay is because of the unrest. "Come back tomorrow and see."

Are you kidding me? I don't know anyone here, don't have a phone, or any way out. The terminal is miles from the base, and there are only Iraqi soldiers outside. I'm screwed.

I have never felt this alone in my life. I drag my bags back outside and search desperately for a friendly face. Besides the Iraqis, there are a few contractors being picked up by private cars. They are likely heading to the Green Zone, a place I don't want to go. A big burly guy standing next to a SUV must notice the panic in my face, and asks if I have a problem. I explain the situation, and by divine providence, he is a driver from the Stables.

My new best friend's name is Denny, and he offers to take me over to the military side of BIAP (Baghdad International Airport). Denny explains my only possible way out of Iraq today is through Kuwait on a C-130 military flight. Once in Kuwait, I can catch a commercial flight. With nothing to lose, I jump in the car and we speed away.

As we approach our destination, to the left is Camp Cropper where Saddam and his gang are held. I wave goodbye and wish them luck. Denny drops me off at three large bubble-like temporary buildings alongside the runway. My savior instructs me where to go and what to say. I love this guy.

There are hundreds of soldiers milling about, packs and guns laying everywhere. On the runway sit numerous Blackhawk helicopters winding up their engines. Next to them is a row of C-130 cargo planes. They are beautiful chariots to civilization, if I can get on one. The line for departures moves faster than most commercial airlines, and the guys at the desk are incredibly helpful. The LOA (Letter of Authorization) stating that I'm here on a presidential order and can move around the country, and the required CAC (Common Access Card) puts me on a military plane.

In no time I am booked on the next flight out to Kuwait. What I do there, I have no idea. I just know I'm leaving Iraq.

I drag my behemoth roller suitcase across gravel to a loading area where baggage will be bundled and put on pallets, and transferred to the plane. Adjacent to the loading area is one of Saddam's jet bunker hangars with a nice hole in it, courtesy of our bombers. I join other passengers in a holding pen, where we get an orientation on how to walk in a straight line to the airplane. Complimentary earplugs are highly recommended, but two water bottles are mandatory. Following our guide across the blistering tarmac to the plane's rear cargo entrance, the slow snaking procession of the fortunate departees fails at walking in a straight line.

Inside the plane there are four rows of red-strapped fold-down benches that take up the front half the interior. Two rows have their back to the plane's sides, and two rows are inside facing the sides. Once seated, we are knee-to-knee, and shoulder-to-shoulder. There is minimal room to stow a carry-on bag just under the bench seat. With everyone still sporting helmets and flak vests, it does not portend to be a comfortable flight. An experienced traveler suggests I sit on my vest for added padding, and in the event we take ground fire. Good tip. The helmet can also come in handy in case of airsickness. For convenience, there is a small port funnel that serves as the latrine next to some unlucky passenger.

After the flight crew makes sure we are packed like sardines, the ground crew starts loading bags. The minuscule airflow making its way into the plane is now blocked. The stagnation and rising temperature are already making me queasy. To punctuate the discomfort, once loading is complete the rear door closes. Encased by heat and darkness, we sit and wait in this giant crockpot. Once the plane interior has reached parboil, I hear the gradual winding sound of an engine starting, then the others, shaking the plane as the pilot revs up the turbo props. The sweet smell of exhaust fills the plane interior and overpowers the stale odor of men.

With only a couple of porthole windows I can't really see outside, and I don't want to stare at the people across from me, so I close my eyes and am thankful I am on my way home. The plane slowly lumbers onto the runway where it parks and revs some more. We start moving, and with glacial speed the shake-and-bake express makes its way into the unfriendly sky.

Once airborne, hints of fresh air make its way through the compartment. I still find it easier to keep my eyes closed and consequently doze off. My nap is unexpectedly interrupted when the plane makes a series of up-and-down hard turns this way and then that. The guy next to me says we are over an area that has encountered previous surface-to-air attacks, and the pilots are employing evasive maneuvers. I'm just glad I don't have to go to the bathroom. As the plane levels off, we pass the danger zone and have just two hours of smooth flying to Ali Al Salem Airbase.

Landed and waiting for baggage pallets to be unloaded before us passengers can disembark, we find that the Kuwaiti heat is even more intense than Iraq. I'll never again complain about a domestic flight being long or stuffy. Walking off the plane, I delight in a refreshing rush of triple-digit air. Surrounding the tarmac are numerous partially collapsed bunker hangers. These have to be the result of Saddam's invasion of Kuwait and Desert Storm precision bombs. Across the runway, heat vapors make the distant powder blue Kuwaiti C-130 air transports look like mirages.

Ali Al Salem is in the middle of nowhere, eerily quiet, and a great place for a sci-fi movie location.

Large buses greeting us have frosty air conditioning, and after over two hours on webbed benches, the padded seats are heavenly. The bus winds through the narrow roads of the abandoned-looking base. Overgrown parking lots and boarded windows are surrounded by new SUVs parked around the weathered buildings. Like Iraq, there is a lot of disguised activity around places that appear destroyed or uninhabited. The buses take a main highway and drive a short distance before turning at a nondescript dirt road. The bus stops at a wide spot in the empty desert, and we are asked to exit our air-conditioned chariot.

Okay, this is kind of unsettling. Thank goodness, most of my co-passengers are American soldiers. Outside, American contractors ask for our CAC cards and tell us we need to get some entry number and stamp to be in or leave Kuwait. For a moderate fifteen-dollar fee, some local bureaucrat can expedite the process in a few hours, or you can wait a few days. The CAC (Common Access Card) is the vital piece of identification, allowing access to military bases, travel, and eating.

Without the CAC card, I am not a legitimate person. While the bribe is not a brain-twister decision, turning over my identity is. Now I am without a CAC card, or plane ticket to anywhere. This day keeps getting better. Our destination is an assembly of recently constructed hangers, warehouses, and enormous lots of parked military vehicles. The football field-sized temporary buildings house the billeting and transportation desk. I grab my bag and shove the soldiers out of the way.

Not really, but I think about it.

Serving as the hub for military and civilian traffic, the massive building is filled with patriotic banners, camouflage netting, and phones ringing. It's the military's Grand Central Station of Kuwait. There are hundreds of people moving with bags, waiting in lines, and looking confused. Though I'm stressed out, the guys behind the transportation counter handle my situation in stride. I guess if they can move whole divisions through the Middle East, my problem is a lark. They put me on the phone with an American travel agent in Kuwait City who assures me I can get a flight in the morning, and he'll even make the reservation. Then the desk offers a bunk, and secures an early morning bus to the Kuwait Airport.

Did I walk into a Ritz by mistake? I feel like I am getting somewhere. I grab my bags and head out the door to find my tent behind the buildings. Dear God, what happened here? The area resembles a moon outpost. There are two colors, dust brown and drab green. Hundreds of tents, each with an umbilical line to an air conditioner, are lined neatly before me. Soldiers and contractors trudge through the oppressive heat to some better destination. Once again dragging my hefty roller suitcase across gravel and sand, I find my tent. Inside are bunks, blankets and pillows. The worldly belongings of other travelers litter the area. Duffel bags and packs have underwear and socks spewing out.

It is too damned hot to care about feng shui.

There's a long line at the phone center, a small utility trailer with numerous phone booths, and I have to figure out how to use an international calling card. People waiting for an available phone are giving me the stink eye as I read the instructions and fail repeatedly. Finally I crack the international codes of zeros and ones and everybody that needs to know where I am knows. The basic response is, "What the heck are you doing in Kuwait?" No one seems to be impressed with my fluid alternate plan.

Casing the area for my later dining needs, there's a McDonald's, KFC, and the DFAC. I head for the showers to remove any trace of Iraq, and apply a fresh layer of Kuwait dust. It's too early to sleep, so I brave the heat and venture back out to see what the immediate area has to offer. I find the obligatory overpriced gift shop of supposed local trinkets. I can't think of anyone who would appreciate a tacky hand-carved camel that was likely made in Indonesia. Next is the PX where all the hats and t-shirts proclaim Kuwait. I scoff at such attire, so far from the hell of battle. Like I'm big stuff just returning from Iraq.

Evening comes and the temperature hasn't lowered by much. Troops are mustering outside under dim amber lights getting instructions on their destination. These guys are headed out to do the real work. I gaze in awe at them, marveling at how young they are, and wondering how many will actually go home one day. With that happy thought I head back to my bunk and try to get some sleep. The same lonely clothes lay about, with no owners in sight. My CAC card should be ready in a few hours, and I have to report at two in the morning to get on the airport bus.

Despite not having much rest since starting, I am awake in a few hours, anxious about what obstacles lay ahead. In the darkness, just outside my tent there are more soldiers lining up. We are going opposite directions. To great relief, my CAC card is ready with the authorizing scribble on the back. I arrive so early at the boarding location that I begin to doubt I'm at the right spot. Fortunately, people start dragging in and we all wonder together.

At the designated time, the buses show up and we board. I am on my way to Kuwait City.

There's not much to see in Kuwait at night. There are smatterings of lights and a lot of black. But soon, the pockets of lights become steady, and we are at the airport. Everyone gets off the bus and heads somewhere, but my airline counter is closed. I have the travel agent contact number, but can't call, because the phones only take Kuwaiti money. So I wait. The feeling of isolation and despair is getting all too familiar.

Finally, an agent appears at the desk. True to his word, the American travel agent has reserved a ticket for me. Whatever the cost, I have to be on the first flight to Jordan in hopes I can connect to my existing reservation. If there are no delays, it appears my travel stars may align. I can't believe it has only been a day since standing with my jaw on the ground at the Baghdad airport.

Hanging from the terminal's main ceiling are large banners of the Kuwait royal family. The terminal is filled with everything from cheesy knockoffs to high-end stores. But I am on a mission to get to my gate. But hark! In the terminal is the biggest Starbucks I've ever seen, two stories high and with a balcony. Temptation is cruel, but I can't take the risk. At security, my CAC card has magical powers, and I proceed swiftly to the gate as the only white guy on the plane.

The quick flight to Amman can't get there soon enough. To make my existing connection back home, I can't afford any delays. Once we land, short of pushing women and children aside, and again denying the sirens of Starbucks, I sprint towards my gate. I don't even care if my bags make the flight. My gate is just beyond security and I am prepared to make a run for it, despite the armed soldiers. But today the sun is shining on me, and I am at the check-in counter. Feeling funky and exhausted, I'm also rather proud of the journey to make this eleven-hour flight.

Once we reach safe altitude, I call home at six bucks a minute. But it is worth it. My wife has no idea where I am, or if I'm traveling by camel caravan. She is thrilled that I am on my way. The thought of being home in half a day is unbelievable. I am a world away from the harshness of Iraq. As I gaze out the window I reflect on what I have seen, the people I have met, and wonder what will happen to them.

Over the next few months I revel at being home with my wife, seeing colors, vibrant vegetation, and playing with my dogs. Like most Americans, I don't really think about Saddam's trial these days. The court's erratic schedule is difficult to follow, and the same rants appear as a snippet buried on the evening news. I fall into the routine of being consumed in my own little world, not with the daily strife or crimes in Iraq. It was a unique experience and I made it home, that's about it. Other members of the original production team follow my exit, but a few diehards remain. While some new crewmembers have agreed to specific time frames, most replacements seem to be open to staying until eternity.

PART TWO

Chapter 14

Back To The Sandbox

My domestic tranquility is broken when I receive a phone call asking me to go back to Iraq. I gladly handed the keys to Baghdad to my replacement, but now he wants a month off for his annual trek to the Indianapolis 500. The temptation of boldly going back to danger, boredom, and a steady paycheck is beyond my willpower. Besides, I am curious to learn how the trial has progressed, and to see my Iraqi friends.

My wife surprisingly understands, which probably indicates I have been around the house long enough. So the decision is made: it is back to the Cradle of Civilization. I will be the one with Stupid stamped on his passport.

Efficient preparation for this kind of trip seems to be elusive. My body armor and helmet are scheduled to arrive by air freight in Los Angeles shortly before my scheduled flight to London. Just before I need to check in, I learn that my armor missed its plane and won't arrive for four hours. This delay causes me to reschedule for a much later flight; however, once in London, my connection time will be relatively brief. So instead of having a long layover at the worldly Heathrow Airport, I can watch American tourists in shorts and sandals for close to twelve hours before I go anywhere.

From London, I travel to Kuwait City where I am supposed to meet "someone" at the airport's downstairs Starbucks. Even though I appreciate the meeting place, I don't have a name of who I'm looking for. My instructions are: "Look for a group of

Americans." Upon arrival in Kuwait I have additional concerns. I still have not received a current Letter of Authorization (LOA) giving me clearance to travel into Iraq. Though for bluffing purposes, I am carrying the old embassy photocopy of the presidential directive. The scribbled authorization on the CAC card from my last trip seems to impress Kuwaiti security, so that is a bonus. The bigger concern is my luggage, which hasn't arrived from London.

I am assured my bags will come on the next flight … in two days. Kuwait must mean "*You* wait."

Without any recourse or clean socks, I sniff my way to the Starbucks and find no one looking like my contact. I'm early, so I head to a business center next door to check my email in anticipation of the LOA. Technology is wonderful, and my clearance is waiting. With fresh copies in hand I can now enjoy a coffee and hope that somebody comes to claim me. With anticipating eyes I look at each group of people coming into Starbucks. They seem to be oblivious to me and content with their conversations. Traveling alone sucks. Without any announcement or prompt, other customers start gathering.

Trying to look like I know what I'm doing, I get up to eavesdrop. Yes, this is it, the group going to the charming but climate-challenged tent city and airport of Ali Al Salem.

The last time I took this ride was in the middle of the night. This time, I can actually see what Kuwait looks like. It looks better at night. On one side of the long stretch of highway are enclaves of massive three- and four-story homes packed next to each other. There are no yards to speak of since it is too damned hot outside.

Each community has numerous minarets pointing towards the sky, and ornate water towers that can be seen miles away.

On the other side of the road is vast open space dotted by circus-like tents of various sizes. Scruffy wild camels freely roam the unfenced wasteland. Luxury cars and recreational quads are parked outside some of the larger tents. I'm told affluent Kuwaitis use these places as retreats to reacquaint with their heritage. But not all Kuwaitis are wealthy, and the less fortunate actually live in the less regal tents. Instead of a Mercedes parked outside, they have goat pens.

Once at Ali Al Salem I make my way to billeting to get my own tent space. I'm not looking to reacquaint with my heritage, just my luggage. Failing to even consider the consequences of bringing alcohol into Kuwait, I had stashed some British Airways wine in my bag.

When I offer the bottles as a gift to the guy behind the billeting desk, his eyes bulge out. "How the hell did you get those here?" he gratefully whispers. He takes the bottles and hides them. Though he didn't remember me, he is the one who helped me find an English-speaking travel agent my last time through Kuwait. It is worth the risk sometimes to bring a little sunshine, or alcohol, into someone's day.

My first stop is to the PX to buy underwear, socks, a towel and soap. I am in a strange land without any fresh clothes, and there is no telling when that will change. Until my luggage arrives, I am stuck in Kuwait. I spend the next day trudging through the heat and dust, aimlessly drifting between my tent, the PX, and eating. For variety, I even sit in billeting to watch the arriving troops. There is literally nowhere to go and nothing to do. If I wasn't so bored, I might feel sorry for myself, but who would care?

The next morning I eagerly take the early bus back to the airport to wait for the arriving London flight. Thankfully, the bags are there. Back at the base, I try to book a flight to Iraq, but fate slaps me once again. It is Thursday, and I discover there are no Baghdad flights on Thursday.

My next option is an early Friday flight that looks pretty attractive, considering the mind-numbing experience here. At this point I haven't slept much in a couple of days, and this night is no different. As per military protocol, nobody seems to know when a flight will leave. This means everyone gets to check in around 10:30 p.m., and hang around a huge staging hall and wait for an announcement. Soldiers are lying across folding chairs trying to sleep, while others just stare into space. The large room is too poorly lit to read so I join in on the space-staring.

It takes all my willpower to fight nodding off as the sirens of sleep in the cavernous hall whisper to me. But my fear of missing the flight out of this limbo inferno makes me strong and I resist.

The shuttle bus finally arrives, and all the zombies climb in for the short trip to the airport. It seems that everyone is so tired and bored that they will get on a bus going anywhere. Once aboard the C-130, sleep deprivation overpowers the discomfort of being tightly packed, and I finally let down my defenses and allow myself to doze. Never mind the stuffy plane, or the pilot's acrobatic defensive maneuvers; I am perfectly content being wedged between burly men for a few hours. By now I'm a pro.

After landing in Baghdad, I again face trying to move from the airport to the embassy just seven miles away in as short a time as possible. It is really crazy to be so close to a destination and be without a safe way to get there. By road, the only way into the city is still Route Irish, and that remains a dangerous and controlled highway. Since it is early morning, the Rhino run won't take place for nearly twenty hours, and I have no desire to wait that long. This time the transportation angels show favor and bless me with a ride on one of the Blackhawk helicopters sitting on the tarmac. The chopper carries about five passengers and their bags, besides the crew. Once more I am embarrassed by the size of my suitcase, but hey, a guy has to look sharp.

As we load onto the helicopter, I am fortunate to score an open door seat—next to one of the two gunners manning 50-caliber machine guns. We are traveling with another helicopter, and they assume a staggered position once airborne. Never reaching more than two hundred feet high, the helicopters fly tight and fast, zipping over the outer reaches of the city. While the gunners warily survey the ground, I lean out for a better view as we approach residential areas. Over outlying farmlands, then reaching streets and neighborhoods, we pass low enough to see the faces of people on the ground. Specter-like women in abayas walk purposefully, never looking up. There are burning piles of trash, stripped automobiles, and decaying homes.

Though tired date palms provide the only color to Baghdad's various shades of brown, it is enough to relegate the city to garden-spot status in comparison to Kuwait. As we cross over the Tigris there is a large park, picnic areas, and tied-up boats around a man-made lake. At one time this must have been a popular place to bring families. Now, it is no doubt too dangerous, and only a sad reminder of happier times. Familiar areas of the Green Zone appear as we pass over the courthouse, 14th of July Bridge, and approach the embassy landing field. The fascinating air tour of the Red Zone ends all too soon with not one shot fired.

Nothing much has changed around the embassy compound. After traveling, there is a surreal familiarity and comfort being back where I know things are. It doesn't take long to start running into co-workers and Iraqi friends, who are all glad to see a face fresh from the outside world. Not that I'm that fresh: I've been wearing the same clothes for five days and had one shower.

Whoever jokes that we should just nuke these countries and turn them into a wasteland should note that God beat everyone to it. Late spring is not the Baghdad tourism season, as the temperatures hover routinely around 120 degrees. Mix that with the gentle desert breezes carrying dust, smoke from burning trash, and you have the makings for a fine afternoon. Supposedly it reaches 140 degrees in Basra. No wonder the locals don't bother bathing. But after Kuwait, I laugh in the face of this weather. However, if I lay by the pool, I'll use BBQ sauce instead of sunscreen.

I am taking the bunk of the guy I am replacing, who took over my bunk when he replaced me, which means I am back in the same bed. At least I won't get lost trying to find the bathroom in the middle of the night. The other half of the trailer is occupied by a crewmember who always has a curtain pulled, so it's like he's not there.

During my absence the Internet has made its way to the trailers. This is getting way too cushy. Unfortunately, it doesn't work on my computer. After some troubleshooting, the problem seems to be the router power supply. Despite incredible odds I get lucky and find the elusive guys installing the units, and they have all the answers. Turns out the fluctuating electricity going into the trailers is blowing up the router power supplies. They've had to replace seven hundred of them so far. They give me a less discerning power unit and I am connected to the world. Of course, young soldiers will undoubtedly follow the accompanying pamphlet warning against accessing Internet porn in an Islamic country and over a government portal.

On the morning before court, I see Senator Orrin Hatch, a troop supporter, at breakfast. I also run into one of the Iraqi attorneys working with our department and he gives me a big hug. He is so proud that the court will take on the rigorous schedule of three days a week. We'll see how that goes. If it is true, as far as court goes, this brief stay will overshadow my previous four months.

Chapter 15

Baghdad Soap Opera

Three months of being home disappear as I enter the court complex. Did I really leave? The barbed wire, blast walls and metal detectors are all too familiar. Even the gate guards recognize me. Up the long flight of stairs, there are no longer bored Iraqi guards posted on each floor. A pretty Russian girl manning a new backscatter X-ray machine outside the courtroom has replaced them. The machine is so sensitive that it detects a vitamin in my pocket. The courtroom interior hasn't changed; no one has installed a gallows yet. The court viewing area is nearly empty as the trial slogs into routine; the number of reporters and spectators watching is drastically diminished.

The television crew seems happy to have me back. I surmise it's just boredom, and not my captivating personality. I am extremely impressed with the stash of snacks they have accumulated for long court days. There's a table of cookies, chips, popcorn and sodas. I fire up the coffee maker with a batch of Starbucks I brought from the land of the free. I'm not terribly disappointed to learn I'm the only one drinking coffee.

The defense is presenting its case in the Dujail case. The court estimates there are two weeks left of witness testimony and that is it. The case then moves to a reviewing court, then passes to a sentencing court. Yeah, there will be a lot of suspense there. Hypothetically, the Anfal trial (gassed Kurds) will start in August or September, but it is dependent on the Iraqi schedule. Regardless, without scheduled court dates it is going to be a long, tedious summer for our crew.

While improvements have been made to courthouse security, order in the court has not been restored. After the defendants are calmly seated and the trial starts for the day, a female lawyer for Saddam instigates an argument with Judge Ra'ouf, and repeatedly insults the judges. Ra'ouf counters with his own tirade and orders her removed. Not to be deterred by expulsion, the attorney rants and points her finger at Judge Ra'ouf. In disgust, she removes her attorney robe and throws it in the direction of the judge. She is literally dragged out by guards, screaming as she goes. We are told by one of our translating attorneys that the female defense attorney was once involved with one of Saddam's sons. We don't know if it was by choice.

Judge Ra'ouf kind of has that look of "Now, where were we?" A defense attorney for Awad al-Bandar, better known in the control room as "Dr. Evil," calls his witness. As president of the Revolutionary Court, the judicial branch under Saddam, Awad never saw a defendant that wasn't guilty, until he became one. Today his former law clerk is testifying the court was independent, and that Awad stayed out of the procedures. Unfortunately for Awad, the former judge's signature is all over scores of death sentences relating to Dujail.

After an attorney meltdown and one unconvincing witness, Judge Ra'ouf adjourns for the day. We're not in session long enough for me to drink a pot of coffee. Other witnesses scheduled for the day have suddenly changed their minds and refuse to testify. We'll resume this legal spectacle in two days with a familiar face on the stand.

Tariq Aziz, the next witness, is truly a celebrity. Synonymous with Saddam's Ba'ath Party regime, the feisty foreign minister is known for appearing on television mocking the West, and taunting the world during the invasion of Kuwait. Aziz's presence in court is a far cry from his diplomatic arrogance and signature tailored suits, as he sits in the witness box sporting a frail look and a hospital smock.

While Aziz is here to testify for Barzon, he makes a point to also advocate for Saddam, explaining that Hussein's government reacted appropriately in trying to suppress an assassination attempt on the country's leader. Aziz illuminates prior violent acts by the outlawed group associated with the assassination attempt, and questions its ties to Iraq's current government.

As probably the smartest guy in the room, Aziz is referring to the Dawa Party, of which the Prime Minister of Iraq Nouri al-Maliki belongs. By connecting the Shi'a dominated political party with violence against the former Sunni government, Aziz is speaking to the faithful insurgency. Aziz also likens Dujail to the way the United States treated the purportedly "unarmed" demonstrators of Fallujah. He finishes his testimony praising Saddam and Barzon.

Not content to let things end on a somewhat positive note, Barzon rises with "I have a story to tell...." This never ends well or quickly. After Judge Ra'ouf has heard enough he shuts Barzon down, and the bickering escalates. Then a defense attorney accuses the judge of being just like an Arab ruler. It's okay to call the court "daughter of a whore," but don't equate the ethnic Kurd Ra'ouf to an Arab ruler. The attorney is sternly told to watch himself. The defendants don't want to touch this one.

While a powerful witness for the defense, Aziz could not explain away the torture and devastation heaped upon the people of Dujail, or the execution of one hundred and forty-eight conspirators. Aziz has been in custody for three years after surrendering voluntarily, and his cases will follow the Anfal trial.

With court recessed for the next few days, my main focus will be trying to survive the heat. Just in walking back to my trailer, I know what a TV dinner feels like. Thank goodness for the trailer air conditioners. The trailers we sleep in are basically storage containers with a bathroom. Made of corrugated metal sans insulation, the trailer (some call it a "hooch") is freezing in winter and baking in summer. About ten days a year the trailer is just right; this isn't the time of year for any of those days. I don't like to waste power and cool the air when I'm not there, but I pay dearly for my conservation efforts.

When I return and crack the door, well, it's akin to opening a 425-degree oven and having your face too close. However, in a few minutes the mighty air conditioners in each unit can change the environment into something fit for a penguin. The process of creating a frosty bliss drowns out all external noises, so I could miss a full-on invasion of the embassy grounds. And though the rumbling fan makes it difficult to watch movies on Armed Forces television, I don't really need to hear the dialogue of *Terminator*.

Finally, though, there is something worthwhile on television: the grainy black-and-white video of an airstrike taking out terrorist Abu al Zarqawi. This is big news in Iraq. Colin Powell referred to Zarqawi as the link between al-Qaeda and Saddam. Zarqawi knew Osama bin Laden, but there has never been proof of his working with Hussein. After being mentioned at the United Nations, and having a $25 million bounty put on his head, Zarqawi became the stuff of terrorist legend by executing spectacular bombings in Amman and Madrid.

Zarqawi was a poor dropout thug with a record of weapons, drugs, alcohol, and sexual assault. After time in prison, Zarqawi wanted to do something positive with his life, so he ran off to join the jihad. Finding his calling in the Mujahidin, Zarqawi finally hung out with enough of the wrong people to get recognized internationally. He has been a real troublemaker throughout the region since.

Our culture refers to people by their last name. Arabs typically go by their first name, and don't emphasize the father's surname, tribal name, or place of family origin. For example, there are people around here with the last name "al Baghdadi." You get three guesses where they are from. By the time Zarqawi was eighteen, both of his parents had died, and he changed his name. Zarqawi's real first name was Ahmed, but he changed it to Abu, after Mohammed the Prophet's successor. Obviously Zarqawi had great plans for himself. His given family name was al Khalayleh, but he also changed that to reflect the Jordanian town where he grew up, Zarqa-hence Zarqawi.

I suppose the rest of his family didn't mind he changed his name, especially since he had moved from common criminal to wanted terrorist. However, in this part of the world, that is a badge of honor.

Back at court, sure there's a trial going on, but there is also love, or just yearning. One of the guys on our crew has a major crush on the cute Russian security girl outside the courtroom. She loves coffee, so I make it and try to get this guy to take it her, but he's too shy. I end up taking the coffee down to her and getting the bonus points, which does me no good; I'm married and old enough to be her father.

Saddam's half brother Barzon can always be counted on for a disruption, even during his defense presentation. This time Barzon gets up and begins his "My Version of World History" statement, and the judge won't have it. While Barzon hasn't had any questions for witnesses all day, the need to spontaneously pontificate is too strong. The judge orders him removed. As Barzon shuffles his sandals out, a guard gives a little encouraging push, Barzon pauses, and is "encouraged" again. The defense table erupts with accusations that Barzon is being beaten, and in front of the judge! The judge says he doesn't see anything wrong, and he will not allow "Iraqis to beat Iraqis" in his court.

The defendants exclaim, "This court is a farce!"

The next day Barzon has wrapped himself in bandages from his "wounds," but is not allowed in court wearing them. The defense pleads with the judge to prosecute the guards and do something about this torture; they claim the abuse occurred in another room and the judge couldn't see it from the bench. The judge reminds the defense attorneys there are cameras everywhere, and anyone who moves in the building is being watched and recorded. The judge tells the defense he had anticipated the claim and had already watched the replay. Ra'ouf says he did not see Barzon hit anything, and nothing hit him. It's obvious to everyone the defense knows there are security cameras, and Barzon has no injuries, but they are just making a show for the media.

Judge Ra'ouf offers to step down if the defense can provide actual proof of injury. If the defense wants to pursue this issue and can't provide proof, they will be punished. The motion is instantly dropped.

Testimony of several relatively credible defense witnesses includes finding a hidden cache of weapons, political items after the assassination attempt, and that residents received compensation for their losses. One witness, governor of the region at the time, claims to know everything about the Dujail event and Saddam's innocence. When Ja'afar presents a document implicating the witness in some of the crimes, the witness changes his tune and maintains he was just a "simple employee." Defense attorneys actually object that the prosecutor is not being "fair" by exposing the defense witness as lying. Yet the defense has one more card to play, and it is a real joker. Additional witnesses testify that prosecutor Ja'afar was in Dujail during a 2004 memorial, and attempted to bribe them into falsifying their stories about Saddam. In fact, the defense proclaims they have videotape showing the prosecutor! The next witness identifies a man pictured in a brief, fuzzy, shaky video as the prosecutor praising the assassination attempt. Ja'afar stands and objects, claiming he has never even been to Dujail.

After a break, Ja'afar calls a surprise prosecution witness into the courtroom; it's the prosecutor's kind-of-lookalike from the video. The defense witness on the stand is forced to admit the man in the video is not Ja'afar, but a man who helped organize the memorial service. The defense effort at a "Perry Mason Moment" fails miserably, and they must concede Ja'afar was not at the event. I mean, did these guys really think that goofball idea was going to work? Obviously, they have no shame.

The next witness self-implodes when he says Ja'afar also tried to bribe him, and starts to read a list of people he personally knows that were not really executed as the prosecution asserted. Judge Ra'ouf demands the list, and then tells the witness to write the names again. The witness is unable to recite one name. Ra'ouf asks the witness where the list came from, and the witness says it was given to him. Oh well, so much for taking the "promise to tell the truth, so help me Allah" oath.

An unhappy Ra'ouf orders the recent defense witnesses held for further investigation. As we bask in the glow of the day's sterling presentation of defense witness integrity, court is adjourned.

According to sources, a hearing is held two days later and the retained defense witnesses admit they are neither from Dujail or attended the memorial services, but had been offered compensation for their testimony. Supposedly Saddam's attorney, Khalil al-Dulaimi, had a hand in this charade.

Even though the defense still has more witnesses, Judge Ra'ouf tells them they have offered enough, and besides, it won't make any difference. Ouch. Trial testimony is finally over.

In three weeks the court will hear closing arguments, so I have had my last scheduled trial day.

The most fun comes from watching an American attorney that began sitting in on the back row of the defense side. We named him the "Professor," because he just had the look of a law school instructor trying to interject himself into a high-profile trial to get some face time, and make his students watch as homework. Sure enough, he turns out to be a visiting professor from a West Bank law school. Listening to his personal interpreter (not the excellent ones furnished by the court), the "Professor" smirks and shakes his head during testimony, like he is ready to spring some precedent-setting legal trap. The cliché expressions are overacting at its worst.

Occasionally the "Professor" stands up and tries to lecture the judge about how international courts work everywhere else. I'm thinking, 'Hey Clarence Darrow, we are in Iraq, during a war, and they don't care.' Plus, after addressing the court in English, he receives repeated admonishments that the court's official language is Arabic. You'd think a well-researched international lawyer would know that. Finally at the end of a day, the guest attorney is given a chance to speak. The "Professor" is so anxious about his great moment he is mispronouncing simple English words that confound his interpreter.

Judge Ra'ouf speaks enough English to be amused, and watches the lawyer vainly attempt to impress everyone. Even Saddam jokes to the judge that this really is an international court now. That's not good when the criminal you represent pokes fun at your grand flourish. This guy doesn't get the hint that he is boring the entire world until his interpreter gets tired, doesn't know certain legal translations, and can't keep up with the conversational flow.

The judge has had enough and tells the law teacher to stop treating them like some class. Ra'ouf then proceeds with an absolutely brilliant dressing-down of the attorney. Exasperated and obviously disappointed with his fifteen minutes of fame, the "Professor" slumps back into his chair. Grade D. He failed, but at least he showed up.

Chapter 16

Summer Camp Ends

Today is an impromptu court hearing, with Saddam appearing solo to answer some questions. The court has a problem in that his attorney is traveling from Jordan, and Saddam is rightfully refusing to answer any questions. This is just another example of the IHT scrambling everyone for a pointless exercise. There is a lot of activity and added security when I get back to the Embassy. In fact, there is a long line forming just to get into one of the entrances.

Upon further inquiry, I learn President Bush has surprised everyone and is here.

After meeting with Prime Minister Al-Maliki, the president is holding an informal reception for the Embassy personnel in *my* coffee shop. There is only so much space available in the room, so I grab a place in line. Just coming back from court I don't have my camera, and I don't want to make the trek to get it, so there will be no Kodak moments. Cell phones are not allowed, so I hand mine off to a friend who's not a Bush fan. Once inside, the room is packed with military anxiously waiting to see their commander in chief. The Secret Service is everywhere, but they're not half as imposing as some of the Marines.

With little introduction, President Bush enters the room to thunderous applause. He is tan and fit, and more handsome than I imagined. The president seems comfortable with the sympathetic audience as he cracks Saddam jokes. I realize I am one of a handful of people who can say they saw Saddam Hussein and President Bush in the same day. For the next thirty minutes Bush captivates the soldiers with words that highlight sacrifice and hope. I want to believe the president when he says that Iraq will set a "hopeful example" to neighboring countries, and their people will demand those same conditions and freedoms. Applause erupts when Bush mentions al Zarqawi's demise. Bush renders a somber prophecy when he tells the crowd that "right now, the world can turn one way or the other."

The biggest applause is reserved for Bush pledging the U.S. will stay and finish the mission. After the speech, Bush wades amongst the troops, shaking hands and posing for pictures. Hundreds of soldiers create a rock-star-worthy madhouse crush to get close to the president. I won't know how long the lovefest continues, I have to leave to retrieve my phone for the scheduled call from my wife. Bush may be the world's most powerful man, but in my world there is a more powerful woman.

During this stay, I'm spending a lot more time talking with Iraqis about conditions here, before and now, what their perceptions are, etc. To them, this is just a big mess that needs a different strategy, or conditions are just going to get worse. Staying the course is not going to improve anything, but prematurely pulling out our troops will be disastrous. Despite our best intentions, all the good deeds and humanitarian aid will go ignored, and foreign military patrols won't bring control to the streets. The Sunni believe Iran is behind the insurgency, and the Shi'a think the Sunnis are to blame. I think it is both. Then toss in the recent introduction of al-Qaeda in Iraq, and Iraq is a stewpot of hate.

To be sure, the surrounding Arab states do not want to see a democratic Iraq succeed. These Iraqis believe their country will understand a strict government and respect forceful military action. So evidently the Iraqi people desire exactly what they were just "liberated" from—a democracy based on fear and oppression. My new friends wish all Americans could see Iraq, and recognize that at one time they laughed, they went to parks, and had a future. They don't envy mega-malls or our way of life. They love and take pride in their country. Iraq is just desperate for any kind of security and peace.

During Saddam's secular regime women could appear in Western attire. But under the threat from insurgents, that is no longer the case. Taliban-like warnings flood Baghdad advising adherence to proper Islamic dress and conduct. Two weeks ago, male members of the Iraqi National Tennis Team were murdered for merely wearing shorts. Radical clerics who feared Saddam's rage now take advantage of new freedoms in speech and the West's ignorance to the jihadi mindset.

As with the Vietnam War, or American Indian conflicts, we don't fight like the natives. Hopefully the new Iraqi military is allowed to deal with their people in a reasoned and controlled manner. Regrettably, beheadings and kidnappings are part of Arab culture, and we won't ever change that. If the U.S. experiment fails here, Iraq could plunge into the darkness of Islamic extremism that may well engulf the entire region. As President Bush said, "The world can turn one way or the other."

While talking with my wife this morning about the president's speech, an explosion interrupts the conversation. It's sickening to hear that awful sound of death and destruction. A roadside bomb near a mosque kills an Iraqi policeman and injures another. The immoral and cowardly insurgents routinely target and make prime examples of the brave new recruits in the Iraqi police and military. Somewhere in Baghdad there is a grieving family, a father who isn't coming home, and a friend that will never laugh again. This indiscriminate viciousness is so foreign to our way of life, and is something I'll never forget when I walk down the tranquil streets of home.

I can leave Iraq reasonably assured Saddam and his cohorts will not be acquitted and set free in my absence.

With truth and justice preserved, I try to take in all the ambiance I can during my final days. As in any war zone, there are some parting memories that are just amusing. Such as a real estate flyer on an Embassy bulletin board offering a Legal House in the Green Zone, 3 Bed, 2 Bath, $7,000.00 a month. On Karaoke Night, as the temperature hovers around 110 in the evening, a person is singing "The Christmas Song" (Chestnuts roasting...). Armored Humvees sporting 50-caliber machine guns display a large sign on their rear bumper that states, Danger Stay Back. On one vehicle someone has removed the "D." Normally I rave about the DFAC (Dining Facility), but then they go and dedicate a night to an Indian cuisine christened "Swarma." I could swear the doctor gave me a shot for that before I came over here.

Then there is Saddam's pool. As the daytime temperature exceeds 120 degrees in the shade, bodies held captive for months inside camouflage uniforms come out to frolic. Culture shock hits the Iraqi maintenance workers who are terribly distracted by the sight of bikinis and so much flesh. Though the female soldiers still are a minority, and despite the various shapes and sizes on display, this is a Playmate pool party to the young Iraqi men. Ever vigilant, a bikini-clad female soldier stands by the pool, a cool drink in hand and an automatic rifle slung over her shoulder. I find that oddly appealing.

Military personnel also throw caution to wind when it comes to skin cancer as they apply gobs of lotion to achieve that desirable Baghdad radiance. After hours baking in the brutal rays, the sun worshipers look like they should be served with eggs and hash browns. The tepid pool water is more wet than refreshing. And there's a Hawaiian Tropic oil slick covering the surface that rivals the Valdez spill. I won't be lowering my mouth anywhere close to this biohazard. Yet, there is something so satisfying and decadent about lounging around Saddam Hussein's pool. Never in Saddam's wildest dreams would he envision himself locked in a cell, and Americans doing cannonballs off his diving board.

Saying goodbye here carries permanence, an emotional significance knowing you will likely never again see or talk to people who have so dramatically enriched your life. An Iraqi national from our RCLO office insists I come to their office and say farewell to the translators. Dr. K (for safety, I'll just refer to an initial) is a PhD who works as a court liaison. We spent hours talking about culture, religion and politics. I actually get teary-eyed over the kind things the translators are saying about my work, my service, and me. The group appreciates that people have come here under dangerous conditions to help Iraqis and their country.

Many are disappointed to learn I don't know when, or if I am returning. I will surely miss these friends from such a different life experience and culture. Dr. K tells me, "You are a true diplomat. I want to tell you that I talk with all the Iraqis, and you are so well liked and respected. Everyone likes you very much." OK, time for tears, hugs, and a hand over the heart. Deep down I suspect they are sad because I am the only one that shares Starbucks coffee, and they're amused with my Arabic, but whatever.

I am anxious to return home, though melancholy at the same time believing I will never know their fates, or see them again. Living on the other side of the world, these wonderful people have a dangerous, difficult life ahead.

It's time to shake off the desert dust, check for bugs, and start my 24-hour journey home. This time I know I'm going through Kuwait, because Baghdad's commercial airport is still closed to international flights. The midnight ride on the Rhino is uneventful until our Humvee escort races off too far ahead. The U.S. Marshal chaperone scolds them over the radio: the purpose of the escort is protection, he says, not to alert the insurgents we're coming.

The flight out of Iraq on the C-130 is packed, stuffy, and hot. Been there, done that, enough said. On the ground in Kuwait, I am fully prepared to relive the joys of tent camping on the Ali Al Salem moonscape. But fate smiles upon me, and I get upgraded to some government housing in Kuwait City. I take the scenic bus ride into the city past the wild camel herds and

159

Bedouin tents, and kids riding ATVs through the desert. Despite the withering heat, families are out enjoying picnics under scrubby trees along the highway.

Kuwait City is modern, clean, and filled with dramatic architecture, but the bus keeps going the other way. Passing empty lots, trash, and billboards proclaiming the benevolence of Kuwait's rulers, our bus winds through residential neighborhoods of large windowless houses jammed side by side, until turning into the Kuwait Hilton Resort. Showing my assorted authorization letters, I get my housing assignment and the keys to a three-story, fully furnished beachfront villa. Thank you, taxpayers of America!

My Arabian palace has a handsome marble shower, Internet, big television, kitchen, real bed, and wide windows facing the hazy horizon of the Persian Gulf. And there is a Starbucks about one hundred yards away. My needs are met. Outside it is hot as hell, so the villas all have window coverings that can withstand a thermonuclear blast. The breezes blowing off the gulf have a distinct filling-station odor. As oil tankers sit docked a short piece away, there are fully dressed Arab women splashing in the water with their children.

I am on a coffee mission. A short, expectation filled walk and oh the joy, the comfort, I am home. While the locals are enjoying the day under outdoor misters, the indoors are just fine for immersing oneself in the atmosphere of caffeine heaven.

Two television crewmembers are here as well; they are the unfortunates heading toward Iraq. One is the guy I substituted for; the other is going to Baghdad for the first time. They exude the high of adventure; I am ecstatic to be heading home. We'll see who is happier this time tomorrow. Before sunrise I gratefully board the bus to the Kuwait City Airport along with other government personnel. The half-hour ride takes us through an undeveloped area laden with Patriot missile batteries. Once we arrive, aggressive boys in maroon bellhop uniforms grab every loose bag in sight. It takes courage and perseverance to retain control of my own bag.

This airport experience is nothing like the last time, when I was in total panic. I am on schedule, I have a ticket, and without a doubt time for coffee and people-watching. Kuwaiti men wear the traditional clothing of a long-sleeved "dishdasha," and usually a white, or red and white headdress called a "gutra" or "kaffiyeh." They habitually finger a string of beads in their hands. Some young women, on the other hand, are wearing Western-influenced designer jeans, and a colorful "hijab" headscarf, while the more conservative favor the black full length "abaya." Most of the women's fabrics have intricate gold designs over black or dark blue, and the men's outfits are spotless and pressed.

Even though there isn't a strict dress code in Kuwait, people are expected to dress respectfully and modestly. Compared to the tank top and flip-flop airport culture back home, witnessing this orderly fashion display is really quite beautiful.

After leaving barren desert the rest of the world looks full of color from above. The Mediterranean is a rich, sapphire blue; Europe's forests appear such a deep green they are almost black; England is a giant meadow of soft emerald hues. As I transfer at London's Heathrow I am on autopilot, going from point A to B. People are moving so fast, and I seem to be moving in slow motion. The change in culture and environment is overwhelming, and almost a sensory overload until I board my plane. The flight seems to take forever, like the plane goes airborne and waits for the Earth to revolve under it. At last I see my wife, and she applies a vise grip on me until we get home.

PART THREE

Chapter 17

Can't Get Enough

It has been three months since I left the desert heat of Iraq. Ironically, I find myself covering a Las Vegas criminal trial during August. Though I have heard rumors concerning a crewmember issue in Baghdad, I hadn't thought much about it. Until I get the call. That person is being removed for disciplinary reasons, and a replacement is needed immediately. Without ample time to get the necessary clearances, let alone find someone with the skills, I am the likely choice.

This is not an easy call home: "Uh dear, will you mind if I go back to where people are lobbing mortars?" While my wife is understanding and agreeable, she has concerns about who will mow the lawn.

So the decision is made: I'm heading back for a third and final encore performance in the Cradle of Civilization. Even though this cradle is being rocked, the baby is not in the least happy. Sectarian violence is rising on the other side of Green Zone walls as Iraqis are getting full-swing into the centuries-old tradition of killing each other. For now, the violence seems confined to Sunni-vs.-Shi'a, and life is pretty quiet inside the gates of Oz.

I leave a signed note for my wife promising this is my last trip.

A several-hour layover in Amsterdam allows me to explore the airport's extensive mall, visit a Rembrandt exhibit, and overhear Europeans talking trash about Americans. At a bar I find some fellow pariahs of mankind who have just returned from Iraq, and listen to their hair-raising tales of installing high-tension electrical wires while being shot at. That beats anything I've done.

The trip to Kuwait is uneventful, meaning my luggage arrives when I do. The next scheduled flight from Ali Al Salem airfield to Iraq is two days away, so I am able to spend a couple of days at the Kuwait Hilton in the nice beachside villa, just steps from a Starbucks. I still can't bring myself to swim in the aromatic water, since the beach is a tee shot away from oil tankers. Of course, oil doesn't deter the vacationing Kuwaitis; to them it's like swimming in money.

Flying into Baghdad in C-130 is a drag no matter how glamorous it may seem. Staying up all night for processing, packing into a flying cattle car with a bunch of hygienically challenged people in stifling heat, and surviving the evasive maneuvers that lift everyone out of their seats and throw them against each other. Military travel is not all the recruitment brochures make it out to be, unless you happen to be an attractive female. Prior to the flight I run into a girl (I'll call Miss T) from our RCLO office, returning from vacation. As the plane is being loaded shoulder to shoulder with personnel, one of the pilots comes back and invites Miss T to ride in the cockpit. Sometimes life is unfair.

I spend my first few hours at the Baghdad airport trying to arrange for a helicopter transport to the Embassy. For some reason, there are lots of troops moving right now. Miss T joins my quest, since neither one of us want to wait all night for the Rhino. We chase the prospect of available helicopters from one base to another, but are repeatedly denied because soldiers have priority. I discover that having a female travel companion has benefits. After Miss T places a few calls, U.S. Marshals send a detail to give us a lift. We happily hop in a monster truck with two heavily armed guards. This truck would make any self-respecting redneck drool. The entire cab is a cocoon of blast-resistant composite outfitted with bulletproof glass. But I am not especially encouraged by the weapons use and evacuation instructions they give us before we hit the road.

The only way from our location to the International Zone is along that most infamous stretch of highways, Route Irish. Oh well, that's only seven miles or so, and traveling at 100 mph can't take that long. I feel a certain sense of imperialistic exhilaration as our convoy tears down the road, lights flashing, guns loaded, and running up behind Iraqis in beat-up Toyotas, forcing them to swerve away to the shoulder. I resist the temptation to wave as the harried drivers struggle to gain control of their cars and shout, "We're Americans, and we are your liberators!"

In all seriousness, the miserable conditions these people live in along the route is just tragic. Everywhere people are digging through trash, and there are too many bombed-out cars and burned buildings to count. It is truly unfortunate that combating the insurgency draws all the resources away from needed humanitarian assistance. But then, agony is exactly what the insurgency has in mind. Anger and desperation are constants wherever the mujahidin import their depraved brand of jihad.

The Iraq version of "Mr. Toad's Wild Ride" concludes at the gates of the Embassy. It just doesn't feel like I ever left this place. Billeting assigns me to a

167

new trailer and roommate; I'll be taking the bunk of one of our crew members that just left, so I already have vital information on my roommate, Charles. The word is he's a nice guy, he knows what we're doing, and could care less. Charles is a Baghdad-born contractor from Chicago who is hardly around, and sleeps a lot when he is. Fluent in Arabic, Charles works in the Red Zone securing police departments, and is privy to a lot more of the danger on the street and war than those of us hiding behind the blast walls.

The first order of business is to shower, then unpack, and maybe take another shower. Once presentable, I'm off to the RCLO office to let everyone see that I can't stop putting my hand on a hot stove. Dr. K greets me warmly: "Thank you for coming back, you are a brave and great man. Once you drink from the Tigris, you will always come back."

Well, I don't know about that. From what I've seen of the Tigris, there's no coming back after drinking that water.

On my way back to the trailer, a maintenance worker earns my nomination for Iraq's most disgusting job. An unfortunate Iraqi man wearing a white plastic body suit, but no mask, is crawling down a manhole to repair the backed-up septic system. With the temperature 110 degrees or so, just wearing a full plastic suit is pitiable. Right now I can't imagine anything more disgusting than submerging into the Embassy's anal cavity. Of course, similar to all maintenance jobs around the world, there are ten potbellied supervisors standing around watching.

Chapter 18

Down to Business

In a miracle of Iraqi jurisprudence the Dujail trial concluded on schedule several weeks before my arrival. The case is now under review by the judges and a decision is forthcoming. No one is expecting a quick decision, because after all, this is Iraq.

The current Saddam Hussein trial is markedly different from the Dujail case. The Dujail trial assistant prosecutor Munqidh is presenting the evidence, and a new panel of judges is presiding over successive days in court. You can imagine the pressure this puts on the Iraqi High Tribunal system, actually having to show up and work. Since my arrival we are experiencing trouble-free full days, with the exception of a defendant becoming entombed in an elevator after lunch.

The Anfal (Spoils of War) trial concerns the mass murder of thousands in Iraq's northern Kurdish province. Between 1987 and 1988 Saddam and his cousin, Ali Hassan al-Majid, employed the use of deadly gases and forms of murder to suppress the rebellious Kurds. While the frequently publicized death toll from chemical weapons is around 5,000, an estimated 160,000 or more fell victim to the genocidal campaign. Everyone has likely seen video footage of the dead non-combatant women and children lying together along the streets. The crimes of Anfal are recurrently shown on the news, and are seen as evidence of Saddam's brutality and willingness to use weapons of mass destruction.

Located in the courtroom is a giant Iraq map flagged with the known locations of executions and mass graves. To get a sense of the magnitude, imagine the saturation of coffee-shop locations in Seattle. At great risk from insurgents and regime faithful, forensic archaeology teams from the Regime Crimes Liaison Office investigated, discovered, and recovered the sights of slaughter. Literally, the entire country of Iraq is littered with thousands of bodies, buried in mass graves where they were executed. Considered "enemies of the state," ethnic Kurd family members were either issued death certificates, or taken and never returned.

This is the trial that should get the world's attention. Ali Hassan al-Majid, Saddam's infamous cousin better known as "Chemical Ali," is here and not afraid to speak. Extroversion must run in the family. Besides Saddam and Ali, there are four other contestants competing for a guilty verdict: Sultan Hashem Ahmad al-Ta'I, a military commander; Husayn Rashid al-Tikriti, a general; Tahir Tawfiq al-Aani, government official; and Sabir Abd al-Aziz al-Douri and Farhan Mutlaq al-Jabouri, military intelligence. And this important trial is not without controversy. The revolving door of head judges continues with the surprising removal of another judge.

Head Judge Abdullah is falling into the same trap as the Dujail judges by allowing Saddam and his gang to intersperse political statements into their witness inquiries. After Kurdish witnesses describe seeing wives, husbands, and children covered in gas dust and dead, the defendants are manipulating their witness questions to introduce complaints about their own deluded injustices. In a statement that shocks the Iraqi viewing audience, Judge Abdullah oddly indulges Saddam, and states that Hussein was not a dictator; those around him had committed the crimes.

That accommodation is too much for the current Iraqi government. A message is sent from the top that they have seen enough.

Under Iraqi law a judge may be sacked at any time, and Deputy Judge Mohammed replaces Abdullah the next day. Around these parts, Abdullah is lucky he only lost his seat. Mohammed is one of the five sitting judges, but we have not shown or identified him thus far in the coverage. That is about to change. The press and defense are quick to criticize the expulsion of Head Judge Abdullah. The press just sees government intrusion, and the defense loses a judge sympathetic to their wrongly accused defendants. In my opinion when the media and the defense are upset about something, that is a positive indicator.

Head Judge Mohammed is less lenient with the defendants, and quickly exerts his authority by removing the unruly bunch from the court on three occasions. This decisive action prompts the defense to walk out and start calling on Iraqis not to accept this court. Yeah, like the country is pulling for Saddam and "Chemical" Ali. In fairness to the former president, five hundred people demonstrate in his hometown of Tikrit. I'm told demonstrations like this happen by either force or compensation.

The parade of heartbreaking witness testimony seems endless. These people have waited a long time to tell their stories, and they are not intimidated. Their memories are clear and their pain is intact. Every Kurdish witness testifies about experiencing the loss of family members, with others suffering the effects of gas, and some tell of holding their dying children. After the attack the remaining Kurds recall walking through their villages and seeing fallen huddled bodies and dead livestock. Survivors are herded up by soldiers and taken to camps. Others make their way to Iran to wait out the purge. Despite years of war with Iraq, Iran offers assistance to the wounded Kurds.

Once at the Iraqi encampments, many are singled out, taken away, and never seen again. In front of the court witnesses freely display their blindness, and visible wounds. Others hold up photos of entire families missing or dead.

On the stand, a woman describes how her husband tried to protect her, and took her identification to show the soldiers. Without provocation, her husband was arrested and taken away. During an exhumation of a mass grave, a wallet was found on one of the corpses. Inside was the woman's identification. As the ID is shown in court, the woman openly weeps. She has not seen the photo of herself since she gave it to her husband. In the faded photograph recovered from the grave she is wearing a necklace that was a gift from her husband. Today, she wears the same necklace during her testimony.

The witness asks if she might have the photo, but Judge Mohammed tells her it is evidence. In an incredible moment, Head Prosecutor Munqidh offers to submit a copy to the court, and return the original to her. But this act of kindness will never make the news.

Saddam, his cohorts, and his attorneys deserve horrible fates. The defendants constantly refer to each other by their former ranks, boast of their importance to the country, and trivialize testimony. If this sounds like the Nuremburg trials, you're right. Hitler is a favorite of Saddam. At the same time, the defense team mocks the witnesses for not having documentation concerning missing or dead loved ones, and attacks the validity of their testimony. After a tearful recollection, a defense attorney has the audacity to ask a witness, "How do we know those were really your family members?"

In the news back home, there is a whole National Intelligence Estimate (NIE) leak and debate thing. The NIE is a report generated by government intelligence agencies that reflects their opinions on things like security and terrorism. Apparently the American media is going nuts over a paragraph taken out of context from thirty pages of analysis. The leaked section names Iraq as a draw and training ground for terrorists, and says that terrorism is spreading and that the Internet is helping distribute the jihadi message. That conclusion is not breaking news or a revelation; it just seems to state the obvious. But the media and some politicians are treating excerpts of this intelligence assessment as some epiphany of epic proportions.

I wish those critical of the report would also be condemning the leak. The publication of an incomplete, yet classified passage, puts lives at risk and aids the enemy. It scares me to possibly be on the receiving end of decisions by an overzealous insider with an agenda. Politicizing security assessments is just wrong and stupid. The problems in Iraq are not a simple task, easily remedied, or walked away from. In the Islamic fundamentalist world there is a very long geopolitical and religious history fueling the anger and frustration. Extremists hate the United States for what we represent, and the threat that it poses to their view of Islam and society.

It is important to recognize that young Arabs are feeling decades of cultural humiliation, economic hopelessness, and social repression. They covet certain Western attractions, and are confused by their own governments and religion. The West is a free society that offers more than is allowed under strict Muslim doctrine. Diversity and choice turns the fundamentalist world upside down; therefore, it must be a threat and it must be stopped. Instead of becoming educated or skilled, the youth are indoctrinated into believing a better life awaits them after death. The present life is bad because of the West. Problems can't be associated with their corrupt governments, and most certainly not Islam. So a rush to join jihad in Iraq or anywhere is no surprise. Freedom of will and thought is the enemy. (To read the history behind the conflict, see the Afterward.)

I will end this rant with a quote from noted Middle East authority Bernard Lewis:

> *It is of course a common phenomenon for members of discontented minorities to gravitate to revolutionary and millenarian movements, in the hope of attaining thereby the equality and opportunities that have eluded them in the traditional order.*

Chapter 19

Anfal Antics

We are sitting and waiting, drinking coffee, snacking, and waiting even more. There is a delay in court starting this morning, and it must be a carefully guarded secret because no one is talking, at least to the television crew. Thank goodness we have satellite TV in the control room. Then the word comes down that the defense attorneys are boycotting the trial due to the change in judges. Here we go again. But justice will not be deterred, and the IHT calls in reserve attorneys who have been watching the case from a holding room.

After the backup attorneys and the judges take their seats, the defendants are brought in. Saddam leads the charge and refuses to accept new counsel, which precipitates the other defendants to follow. The rejection escalates into a shouting match between Saddam and Judge Mohammed. The judge, wanting no part of Saddam's lecture, ejects the former president from the proceedings. So far the day is going just great.

Next come three lackluster witnesses that receive little or no cross-examination. I think even the judges are bored, and realize the futility in continuing under these circumstances, so they call it a day. It really is pointless to conduct the trial when half the courtroom isn't present. We are told we might continue tomorrow, or we might not.

I take the advantage of the short day and head over to the PX. Even though I don't need anything, it's always a good strategy to buy before the need arrives. Sometimes other people think they want the same things I do, or supply convoys are delayed or blown up, and the shelves are bare. Today's exciting purchase is shower soap and mouthwash. I may be in a land of camels, but I don't have to smell like one.

Until the dust settles, so to speak, around the court from the boycott I resume my normally scheduled life of eating, reading, working out, and sleeping. It's not a bad existence if you can block out the environment.

I received an email that I will pass along. I didn't verify if it is factual, so take it as it is:

If you consider that there has been an average of 160,000 troops in the Iraq theater of operations during the last 22 months, and a total of 2,112 deaths, that gives a firearm death rate of 60 per 100,000 soldiers.

The firearm death rate in Washington, D.C. is 80.6 per 100,000 for the same period.

That means that you are about 25% more likely to be shot and killed in the U.S. capitol, which has some of the strictest gun control laws in the nation, than you are in Iraq.

Conclusion: The U.S. should pull out of Washington.

While the defense still has their panties in a bunch, the trial is on hiatus. After covering trials for so many years I have never seen, or thought I would ever see such childish, unprofessional behavior from attorneys. The court's acceptance of these delays is beyond rational thought. Capitulating to the dramatics and manipulation is unfair to the witnesses, and the Iraqi people. The court cannot expect to have any credibility with such a weak hand.

But then, maybe they don't care what people think.

It's anyone's guess why the break is lasting so long. Perhaps it's due to Ramadan, or the judge is giving the defendants time to talk with their absence-prone attorneys, or conceivably, there is some goat-slaughtering festival. In any case, the defense has elected to continue their boycott, so the Kurdish genocide trial resumes with court-appointed attorneys.

The new attorneys seem to actually pay attention and take their situation seriously. From what I am seeing initially, they are asking more relevant questions than the original attorneys. Some of the defendants seem okay with the substitutes, while others ignore the replacement lawyers altogether, and appear resigned.

The Kurds are a fascinating ethnicity for this region. Their characteristics are not Iraqi or really Arabic. They have distinct, handsome features, like high cheekbones, pointed noses, blue eyes, and fair skin. Most show effects of weathering due to their high mountainous region and lives as farmers.

The men wear these wild jumpsuit outfits with really baggy pants, big belt or sash, and a little cap encircled by printed cloth. I'm guessing M.C. Hammer checked these fashions out in a *National Geographic* back in the 1980s. The women wear traditional hijab scarves over the head (they are Muslim), an ornate vest or jacket complementing a flowing, sheer, body-length "garmiyani" or gown, over satin puffy pants. The outfits I see are typically black with sequins or elaborate gold leafing, and some incredible, night blue accents. They are striking and beautiful.

From the northern province of Iraq, Kurds speak their own language and require Arabic translators. So in the control room I am now listening to Kurdish to English, and Arabic to English, to follow what the heck is going on. But the hatred in the Kurds' eyes for

Saddam Hussein is a universal language. Men and women glare at him throughout their testimony, and each finish by asking Saddam why he did such a thing; what had their children or families done to him? They are precise in their facts and are not frightened by Saddam.

They have waited twenty years to tell their stories, and the opportunity to confront the former president face to face is an experience they almost certainly never anticipated. Saddam sits calmly taking notes, and seems uninterested. He barely looks up.

As in any trial I cover, there is a quest for comicality in order to deal with the harsh reality. The lead prosecutor in this case is Munqidh, and he served as an assistant during the Dujail case. One morning, court is delayed and we are informed there is a problem with the television coverage. Just a week into this trial and we are creating an issue? That can't be a good thing. Then the issue is explained. It turns out the prosecutor's family complained to Munqidh that he isn't on TV enough. We are further enlightened that Prosecutor Munqidh is refusing to continue until he has assurances that his face time will increase.

In the middle of a controversial trial where there is a body count of those involved, not enough exposure is a worry? It sounds like an excuse to conceal something else. The general consensus in the control room is that it has more to do with Munqidh getting pushed around during the early trial days by Judge Abdullah, Saddam and the defense. By following the action, perhaps we are showing too much of the discontent, and too little of a strong prosecution. To support this jaded assumption of instability in the prosecution, Dujail

Head Prosecutor Jafar, though not an active court participant during Anfal, comes in and temporarily takes the lead from Munqidh. After a few days under Jafar there is peace in the valley again. For better or worse, Munqidh will get his wish.

With all due respect, I have to make a cheeky observation. While the Kurds are an attractive lot, the testosterone level within the male population must be astronomical. Whatever these guys are eating or doing is the secret that Hair Club for Men has been looking for. Their eyebrows have more hair than my head. Only the strip of black, dense carpet nap disguised as a mustache rivals the bushy caterpillars above their eyes. When the men remove their shirts to display scars on their backs during testimony, the court is subjected to a vision reminiscent of a hefty buffalo hide.

Regrettably, Ramsey Clark, the world's rights protector of dictators persists on holding press conferences in New York. Why any self-respecting reporter attends, or any broadcast outlet considers his views newsworthy, shows how partisan the media can be. Come to think of it, the media probably agrees with his sentiments. This time, Clark is predicting wide spread violence among the Sunnis if Saddam is convicted and sentenced to death. Like uh, Iraq kind of has that already. Besides, the dancing Shi'a and Kurds will make up for it. Though inappropriate, it's a nicely timed advocate maneuver (aka, threat) as the Dujail judges deliberate.

I really do have a great amount of admiration and compassion for these Kurdish witnesses. They have lost so much, and had to wait so long for justice. It is unfortunate that the IHT judiciary impotence, the external violence shrouding Iraq, and bellicose defense attorneys render the proceedings a sideshow. With so much effort put into the trial preparation, evidence gathering, and finding of witnesses, the actual court process is seemingly void, or at least deficient of credibility. One would assume human rights groups might rally to this trial and promote it as an example of a well-documented crime against humanity case. An ethnic cleansing in which the world bore witness and did nothing, again. Instead, the rights groups are concerned about the defendants. Go figure.

But I digress, and the trial continues. Most of the defendants are taking notes during testimony. Saddam's countenance is boorish as he repeatedly and rudely yawns. I guess tales of genocide are old news. Been there, done that. The Kurdish attorneys sitting with us expect Hussein to flip out later this week when testimony detailing encampment rapes is presented. Why Saddam would show increased interest is beyond me. For years Saddam and his heartless sons gained infamy for that brutal activity.

Well the Iraqis may not quite grasp the concept of democracy, but they have the shortened-workweek thing down just fine. Union bosses everywhere should take notice of Iraq's fine example—same pay for fewer hours, non-existent performance expectations, no repercussions for poor performance, and putting first everybody's religious holidays. To top it off, the entire defense council is boycotting the trial and still getting paid.

Case in point: The court is taking ten days off to allow the new defense team to meet with their clients and strategize. When court resumes, IHT's proposed schedule shows us meeting for three blistering days of trial, followed by five days off, then three days of work, then a week off. Phew, let me catch my breath.

I'm spending the break studying Arab culture, writing, and sleeping, which is probably more than the defense team is doing. There is some excitement around our paradise when security uncovers an insurgency plot to enter the Green Zone with explosive vests. That is neither nice nor fashionable. The outside air is particularly stinky, and though Iraqis don't raise pigs, it smells like a livestock ranch is across the street. I can't imagine how the people laying around the pool or eating their lunch out there can take it. At this point, I'm hoping the wind will change and send fumes from the refinery in my direction. With nothing to do and nowhere to go, these long work breaks can feel like a maximum-security prison, except the showers are safe.

After ten days of paid recess, the Anfal trial resumes for a brief, passionate session. The prosecution begins with Kurdish witness testimony that intensely details rape and torture atrocities too horrific to repeat. The numerous accusations and blame will presumably set off Saddam and his gang, who neither want to hear or see the evidence. Obviously, the pot is boiling because Hussein has been giving the judge the stink eye all morning. The scowling former president looks like he's just eaten a bad tuna-fish sandwich. Finally Saddam tires of hearing what an awful person he is, and starts the festivities.

To no great surprise, Saddam embarks on a flattering version of history and rule under his regime. Even though this grandiose oration is exactly what the viewing audience wants to see, Judge Mohammed isn't interested and presses the button that signals us to shut down the defendant's microphone and limit the camera to the judge. By now Saddam has the little red indicator light figured out, and he doesn't like it one bit. The former leader will not accept being told what to do, and he certainly doesn't like losing his televised political forum. Judge Mohammed and Saddam take off the gloves and go at it, though we can only show the judge's side of the squabble.

When Saddam crosses the line and insults the judge by association with members of the animal kingdom, Mohammed demands that Hussein be returned to his cell. As Saddam curses his way to the elevator, the remaining regime gang finds the courage to play follow-the leader. That long break and this new schedule are working out great. Everybody is pissed off, and the defense attorneys and defendants have now both walked out. I wonder if the IHT has substitute defendants?

However, I have to give Saddam credit. Today is a win for him, because who is going to focus on the earlier rape and torture testimony? What will be remembered is Saddam standing up and fighting an unjust, controversial authority. The next day is a repeat more or less, until the skirmish.

Unfortunately for the viewing public, the scuffle between some of the defendants and the Iraqi guards is not televised. After a series of disrespectful interruptions, the judge is already indicating that we are going into a closed session (no TV), and that the boys in the cage will not be staying. As the defendants are being escorted out, tiny Husayn Rashid, a former military dynamo around seventy-five years old, starts swinging and kicking. To the defendants, bad behavior is infectious, so they all get involved in the fray. These former regime thugs don't like being touched, and certainly not manhandled by commoners. The defendants bawl boastfully about how important they used to be, how they ruled for thirty-five years, and how dare anyone treat them like this.

After years of pushing around the Iraqi population, it is a wretched turn of events when the sandal is on the other foot.

Doing their best not to hurt the rowdy geriatrics, the guards are trying to protect themselves from the flailing bony arms. Finally the guards grab Husayn and put his arm behind his back until he cries "uncle." This show of force brings accusations of brutality from the rest. I can only imagine what will happen when the Iraqi guards get these guys out of the judges' sight.

But the next day nobody is wearing a cast or showing visible signs of torture. As a matter of fact, the court has an Age of Aquarius feel. The defendants all come in, sit down, and politely ask to be heard. The pleading defendants just ask for respect, the ability to defend themselves, and they sincerely honor the judge. Huh? What the heck happened down in those holding cells last night?

Then Saddam gets up. Perhaps having some out-of-body experience as well, Saddam now speaks of himself in the third person. It's like I'm watching that Seinfeld episode with "Jimmy." He says "Saddam" wants to be good, but "Saddam" gets upset when he hears lies and distortions. And of course, "Saddam" respects the court and the judge. In this Kumbaya moment, the judge joins in the lovefest and agrees to listen to their grievances, but the defendants have to respect him and the court. I suppose that also means no whispering or passing notes. Thank goodness the judge can't hear what we're saying up the control room.

The glow of sappy unification fades quickly as witnesses with a whitish glaze over their eyes, and sensitivity to light—or blindness from chemical burns—describe horrific events that happened in front of them. Testimony goes beyond the loss of sons or brothers to appalling, sadistic abuses of women and children. In the camps, men were beaten constantly, children were disemboweled, and women repeatedly raped, kicked, and laughed at. The details become so gruesome I have to stop listening. Unfortunately, the villains directly responsible have long dispersed into society and will not face earthly judgment.

But for the criminals that authorized the brutality, namely Saddam and his helpers, the underworld will have a special corner prepared when they get there.

Earlier, I neglected to mention the tattoos that the Kurdish women display. The decoration is strictly tribal, and not some hummingbird-on-the-shoulder sort of tattoo. Drawing inspiration from poor artistry and what must have been a leaky ballpoint pen, the tattoos are lines that descend from the lower lip to the chin. There really is no aesthetic balance to these lines. Maybe they are added to like bonus points as earned. The cheeks may display a rising sun, an indiscernible scribble, or for the lucky ones, nothing. I originally thought the symbols meant ownership or something, but the more attractive women don't have them. So who knows? Saddam has tribal markings on his right wrist that resemble a band, and sports a sun tattoo on his hand. Or maybe he just had his hand stamped when he went to "Salsa Dance Night" at the prison.

To finish out the wacky day, a nearby ammo dump is hit by a mortar around 11 p.m. For over an hour, loud explosions rattle the trailers, helicopters scramble, and incoming warnings blare. *"Danger. Incoming. Stay where you are."* Try going to sleep after that. Oh well, maybe I'll just think about the trial.

There is a special closed hearing today with defendant Sultan (a former general who sits beside Saddam) and his original attorneys. The rest of the defendants and court staff have the day off. Though everyone is speaking in Arabic, it's easy to figure out they are discussing seeing the witnesses more clearly, and the defendants having the ability to speak their minds. The hearing is more discussion than court proceeding, since everyone is pointing and walking around. In usual Arabic fashion, the talking starts calmly, then rises until everyone is talking at once. Then they settle down and act like buddies.

Sultan is smiling and holding his hand across his heart, signifying his sincerity and gratitude. This guy has psycho eyes and a wicked smile, and I just know he could kill in an instant. I wonder how people saw that happy evil face in their last moments.

Once all parties are satisfied and the hearing draws to a close, a cell phone goes off in the court to the tune of "Jingle Bells." That's a festive but awkwardly embarrassing ringtone for a courtroom full of Iraqi Muslims. Today's procedure is not for broadcast, but recorded for the record only. The judges wanted the hearing documented in the event the attorneys, or defendant accused them of demanding bribes, or there was some type of coercion. We also hear from security that Saddam's original attorney is in the building, accompanied by Ramsey Clark. Oh boy.

As we leave the courthouse for the day, fighter jets are heading north. The ominous sound of attack runs lasts for hours.

The atmosphere music and aromatherapy sessions down in the holding cells must be working for the defendants. This morning we have an unusual calm start, with the defendants waiting politely to speak. General Sultan has a new seat behind Saddam. He had been seated in the front row to right of Saddam, but now he is in the second section of the "cage." The "cage" is only about four feet high, with three sections, each having a latched gate. Perhaps Sultan thought Saddam was getting him in trouble in front of the rest of the class.

Prosecutor Munqidh's brother was assassinated yesterday. His brother had been prominent in Saddam's government, but was not a Ba'athist *per se*. Munqidh is present and acting normally, bravely defying intimidation. More Kurds take the stand and tell of seeing people hung upside down and tortured, and a man who had to dig a grave for his wife and baby with his hands.

To Saddam, these old stories are wastes of time. He has something new to say in an open letter to his people. Presented by his defense attorneys, the message implores citizens to stop killing each other, and turn their anger toward the occupiers. I'm thinking, "Gee, thanks Saddam." Shameless defense attorneys who have no problem accepting $1 million retainers from the "occupiers" read this love letter to the faithful, promoting violence against Americans. The letter is signed "President and Commander in Chief of the Holy Warrior Forces." Saddam never led anything holy in his life.

We are in final testimony before the court breaks for another couple of weeks. Maybe the court needs to assemble a fresh batch of witnesses, or perhaps one of the judges has a pre-paid vacation to the Dead Sea. Whatever it is, the IHT just doesn't seem motivated to complete a trial, or give an explanation. The Kurds keep revealing stories more horrific than the one before. On the stand a man describes being herded on to a truck and driven to a trench. Once the Kurds are lined up, the soldiers open fire and fill the trenches with bodies. The witness, while not hit by a bullet, falls into the pile of dead and dying. As the trench is covered, the man removes his clothes so he can blend in with the dirt. After the soldiers leave, the man escapes and remains in hiding until the regime is toppled two decades later. The parallels to Nazi Germany don't end there.

The next witness describes being rounded up with other Kurds. When he asks for water, a soldier tells the witness he isn't going to need it because they are all going to die anyway. Then the soldier throws the water at the doomed souls. The group is loaded onto windowless buses and taken to a camp. During World War II, the Nazis perfected windowless buses, and often had the exhaust piped back into the passenger hold. The witness further describes how camp dogs ripped at the pile of corpses outside of a death chamber.

These graphic, unpleasant descriptions should make the news, but they never will. Instead, there is international concern whether every inmate at Guantanamo has a Qur'an.

During this extraordinary testimony, Saddam affects an odd daydream smile that is inexplicable. It is as if he is recalling fond memories. He seems at peace, and not at all disturbed. Maybe he is reliving those crazy, heady days of invading Kuwait.

As I wait for transportation back to the embassy, I flip on Kurdish television to see if they are reporting today's events. The channel is playing a music video where a man is walking and singing his way through recreations of the Anfal villages being pillaged and burned. Instead of gyrating dancers, the video features panicked women and children running through the streets, and concludes alongside backhoes digging a mass grave. After twenty years these people have not forgotten what tragedy befell them. And I don't suppose there is any chance the media will ask the Kurds what they think about America's recent intervention.

Before we take a break in the trial, I looked into what the defendants do during down times. I mean, can they watch "Golden Girls," or play Twister? The guys can't be getting a lot of visitors since their families all left the country with suitcases full of money, and their close friends are dead or in jail with them. As for an adoring public, well … Saddam really has none.

So, what keeps them busy? Well, from information gleaned from one who would know, the regime elite does crafts, specifically Japanese origami. Apparently, former Foreign Minister Tariq Aziz is the master. The man who often stood before the United Nations now uses plastic tableware and plates to make incredible swans and the like. It's my guess Vice President Cheney has guards watching to see if Saddam will try to secretly construct a Weapon of Mass Destruction out of a plastic spoon and fork. The defendants also take full advantage of the American staffed medical and dental facilities. Considering how they indulged themselves, that alone might break the war budget. Besides, the U.S. wants this bunch healthy for the executions.

Chapter 20

The Verdict and the Reaction

While the IHT languishes in hibernation, there is big news from this region. At a major meeting held in Saudi Arabia, Shi'a and Sunni Islamic clerics agreed to call for an end to sectarian violence in Iraq. The religious edict, or "fatwa," was signed by all attending. The document has been forwarded and approved by the influential Shi'a Grand Ayatollah Ali al-Sistani, and the little firecracker cleric Muqtada al Sadr. Muqtada heads the out-of-control Mahdi Army, a violent, merciless Shi'a gang from the Baghdad slums of Sadr City. Whether the Shi'a insurgency listens is questionable. A major Sunni has yet to sign the agreement. At least it's a step in the right direction.

Also, in a rare criticism of Shi'a resistance organization Hezbollah (Party of God), Egypt's Foreign Minister is blaming the militants for a series of skirmishes with Israel that are derailing the peace process. There are accusations that Iran paid Hezbollah fifty million dollars to detain a captured Israeli soldier in order to provoke Israeli attacks and stir animosity. Iran also just sponsored a pro-Palestinian rally the other day. Sometimes, there is just way too much intrigue to do any good. I wonder if this part of the world is ever happy about anything.

There is troubling news in the Green Zone. An American soldier born in Baghdad and working as an Army interpreter has gone missing from the area. There is concern that he has been kidnapped, possibly while venturing out to the Red Zone. Leaving a base alone, or without authorization, is against regulations and common sense. Though we want to believe we are sheltered around here, walking at the wrong time to some little Green Zone market to buy a dollar movie can prove disastrous. This is a reality check that none of us are immune from "missing." The Iraqi and American forces' intensive manhunt throughout the city is causing objections from the local commerce because of intrusive checkpoints. That's just too bad, sorry for the inconvenience.

I also read about an organization of two hundred U.S. military personnel calling for the immediate withdrawal of troops from Iraq, citing the lack of WMDs and al-Qaeda connections. The spokesperson that was quoted served six months over here. Okay, granted, no WMDs were found, but even Saddam's closest confidants thought they existed.

But there are plenty of other reasons to be here. Let's not overlook the seventeen broken UN Resolutions, Saddam's verbal threats to the United States and its allies, and Saddam's payment to the families of "martyrs" who attacked our country's interests. Then there is the systematic slaughter of the Marsh Arabs after the Gulf War, a group that joined the revolt and paid dearly when Desert Storm ended. And lastly, there is the genocidal Anfal campaign of the Kurds.

Sure, America can't be the world's policeman, but our country has historically become involved when others are repressed. Sometimes the United States is hailed as a savior, other times scorned as a meddling giant. Right or wrong, we are here, and it is a war that needs to be won. So instead of commending the hundreds of thousands of active duty personnel, a meager group of two hundred with a spokesperson that spent a whopping six months deployed is what grabs American headlines. Yeah, there's no bias in the media.

An Air Force morale band is playing tonight in the embassy coffee shop. Its name, High Flight, conjures up a lot of Broadway showtunes. Since I'm not working, I don't have anything better to do but watch. The room is packed with soldiers, way more than the publicized anti-war group. Made up of Air Force personnel, the band is extremely entertaining and skilled. To reach everyone's tastes, they play a variety of country, rock, and soul. But watching the troops' faces brings my greatest joy. They are enjoying the music so much as they watch pretty girls in fatigues sing, and believe for a few minutes they are back home.

Even a three-star general gets up and joins in the singing. Not surprisingly, he receives a standing ovation. There is no visible discord over here. These troops want so badly to be appreciated, to be supported from home, and the ability to finish their mission. I honestly look for negatives in troop morale, and I just don't find it.

Unfortunately the push for a "Cut and Run" policy is gaining traction back at home. It is disingenuous to proclaim support for the troops, but criticize what they are doing. To me it is an honor and privilege just to be around so many brave and courteous soldiers. Political posturing makes the news, and no one asks the soldiers why they are serving. The soldiers believe in their role here, and that is good enough for me. (I forgot to mention to play some patriotic background music while reading this.)

Later, I talk with two of my Iraqi friends. They are so fearful of what will happen to their country should the U.S. leave too quickly. Where can they go? Would another country accept Iraqis? The two Iraqi girls in their twenties—one is Sunni and the other Christian— already have credible death threats as the result of their jobs as interpreters. They can no longer go home at night to see their families in the city, and they now stay in an embassy trailer. They ask me to pray for them.

Despite the heaviness of their burdens, they still manage to smile and have hope. But, I guess we should just pull out and say, "Oops sorry. Our mistake" and let them deal with this mess. Surely the Mahdi Army, the Islamic Army of Iraq, al-Qaeda, Iranian agents, and the Ba'athists will agree to stop when we leave. As I walk back to my trailer the sound of gunfire erupts from across the river, jets streak overhead, and Medevac helicopters bring in the wounded.

After an extended break we resume the Anfal trial for what is supposed to be four days of testimony. However, there are only enough witnesses for two days. Efficiency is not the court's hallmark. But before we restart Anfal, Saddam's original attorney, al-Dulaimi, is making a rare appearance in court to issue nine points or demands concerning Dujail. While al-Dulaimi asks for everything including the kitchen sink, he neglects to ask for Saddam's pardon. The attorney does, however, bring up General Husayn Rashid's bony-arm incident with the guards from a couple of weeks ago. Presenting a visual aid to clarify one complaint, al-Dulaimi shows a four-inch thick binder of document evidence provided by the prosecution. As he displays the binder to the judges we see nothing is legible; every page and line of evidence is redacted. Oops. Al-Dulaimi threatens to walk out again if his demands aren't met. The judge indicates that they will address the issue, and advises al-Dulaimi not have the door hit him on the way out.

The Anfal testimony consists of more family loss, of being blinded by gas, lists of the dead or missing. One witness describes seeing dead children, still clutching candy from the end of Ramadan. After hours of listening to this I find my mind drifting, just tuning it out. It is too horrible and unimaginable to take any more space in my memory. For different reasons, the defendants don't look at the witnesses, react, or ask questions.

One of our translators visiting family in Jordan during the break was shocked to hear their interesting perceptions of the trial. Since Saddam dresses so nicely in court, they believe he must be flying on a private jet every day and returning to his family at night. When the judge hits our red button to cut off audio, they think that Saddam is saying something that makes the judge afraid. Amusingly, they also think the court may be fake, because people from Hollywood could be there manipulating images. Rats, we've been discovered.

Just days from the big verdict, numerous explosions are followed by sirens and gunfire. Most of the explosions happen in the morning and there is actually a reason for that. The rationale is if you become a martyr before noon, you will have lunch with Mohammed that day. Hey, I can't make this stuff up. The Iraqis shared some gallows humor about a suicide bomber who died right at noon. When he ascended and asked to have his lunch with the Prophet, he was told Mohammed had already eaten, but he could "Go and do dishes with Omar." That is some wacky insurgent humor.

194

Sunday is a brand-new day, the birds are chirping, the sun is shining, and we have a verdict reading in the Dujail case. Hmmm, I wonder what it will be? After such a long stretch of killing time, I am excited to actually have responsibilities. I was about to go out and start helping the Iraqi workers sweep sand. It's one thing to have a paid vacation, but quite another to spend it here.

En route to court, there is a conspicuous security presence. I think everyone in the Green Zone knows to avoid this street today unless you have business and credentials. American troops, Humvees, and a tank block the court compound entrance. To my relief, inside the complex walls is another strong contingent of American soldiers. There are more Iraqi guards than usual, but instead of looking like they want to kill us, they are the happiest I have ever seen them. While we go through security, the guards laugh and smile, and we are their best friends. Besides the stench of burning trash, there is a sense of relief and retribution in the Iraqi air. But on everyone's mind is the fact the verdict has not been rendered, and no one really knows how the insurgency will react.

Inside the court, we check all the equipment again. It just wouldn't be proper to have one of the remote television cameras drop on the judge's head as he reads the verdict. But everything is good, coffee is brewing, and there is no incoming fire. As if these judges ever adhere to a schedule, we are told that the start of court is going to be "fluid." For the moment, the delay is due to "personality issues" amongst the judges. To this day, I don't know what that means.

Once the secret mystery issue is resolved, the judges seriously discuss the defense attorneys' request to present some poetry Saddam has just written. I don't know, maybe I mistook "fluid" for "stupid." My adjective confusion is confirmed when the defendants' new seating chart is changed three times before anybody enters the room. Perhaps none of the defendants wants to sit by the ticking time bombs that are Barzon and Saddam.

Some of the defendants enter in an orderly, subdued fashion appropriate for men about to learn their fate. To no one's surprise, Barzon is not one of them. It has been several months since Barzon was in court, and it looks like the jail cuisine has added a few inches to his waistline. Saddam enters with his usual arrogance and disdain. With the exception of Saddam, the defendants wear traditional clothing as a thinly veiled symbol of commonality with the people. It's also a blatant sign to the masses that the "occupiers" are about to condemn poor oppressed Arabs.

The judges enter quickly and Judge Ra'ouf calls for the defense attorneys. He demands they enter the court one at a time so he can see them. I'm thinking this is for the sake of security; they are defense attorneys after all. But the reason is much more dire, because implanted amongst most of the original defense team is Ramsey Clark. I knew this was going to be a good day.

Saddam's lead attorney al-Dulaimi requests a delay in the proceedings that is promptly denied. Undeterred, the attorney then offers the court a brief, written by Ramsey Clark, in a cheerful pink binder. Okay, I am not an attorney, but I know better than to present something that looks like a prop from *Legally Blonde*. I wonder if it is scented as well. Seriously, this defense team is either foolish, flippant, or both.

Judge Ra'ouf tells the defense he has already read Ramsey Clark's brief and isn't impressed. Ramsey is still struggling to put on his translation headphones correctly when Ra'ouf turns his wrath toward the American lawyer. The judge sternly orders Clark removed from the courtroom immediately, and by force if necessary.

Ramsey Clark hesitates and begins to protest just enough to make the guards grab him. Regrettably, we cannot show Clark getting the bum's-rush ejection in its entirety because the cameras would reveal the guards' faces. And right now, I want to buy those guys dinner. Though it may be shallow, I think I just witnessed the most satisfying display of judicial discretion I have ever seen.

The entire defense team and defendants sit and watch the spectacle. There are no further outbursts or disruptions on behalf of the ousted attorney. We are told that Clark's brief contains foul language, and insults toward the judges, the prosecution, and the Iraqi High Tribunal. Offensive, disrespectful wording by an attorney is a gutsy strategy to advocate for the client.

It is finally showtime, and Judge Ra'ouf begins reading the verdicts. The first defendant to hear the news is Mohammed Azawi Ali, who resembles Boris Karloff and looks like he may not live to hear the verdict. But he is acquitted. Azawi will not be celebrating, however, because he has charges pending in future trials.

The next three defendants include the father-and-son combo of Abdullah and Mizhir Ruwayyid, and Ali Diyah Ali "Moley." All three receive fifteen years, but father Abdullah misses the verdict and sentence because his hearing aid stopped working. I hate when that happens. Taha Ramadan, the "Picker" and former vice-president, is given a life sentence. Taha first calls on Ba'ath Party members to fight, then meekly asks the judge how someone so innocent could be convicted. Here's a hint, Taha: It might have something to do with your signature all over the death orders.

Next "Dr. Evil," the former head of the Revolutionary Court, Awad Hamad al-Bandar, receives a death sentence. Throughout the judge's reading Awad is shouting, "God is great." Awad will be able to make his case in person soon enough.

Out of deference to my crew seniority (or age) the other camera operator kindly offers control of Saddam's camera for the verdict. Next is Saddam Hussein, aka the "Lion," aka the "Sword of Islam." The judge is obviously saving the best, Barzon, for last, Saddam does not want to stand to hear the bad news. Judge Ra'ouf dispatches guards to assist the former ruler to his feet. Though he doesn't like being touched, or having his arms bent unnaturally, Saddam wiggles enough to keep the guards by his side. This wrangling is causing me some distress since I don't want to inadvertently show a guard, but let's face it: This is the Kodak Moment.

Finally people take their proper positions and I can squeeze enough zoom out of the lens to eliminate the guards. If they lean into the frame, oh well. Saddam stands stationary, ready to take his verdict like a man.

As the death sentence is read, Saddam defiantly shouts his predictable buzz phrases, "Death to the enemy of the people!" and "Long live Iraq!" He needs to print that stuff on t-shirts for his appeal fund. With contempt and a fierce scowl, Saddam is in full bluster standing at the cage's podium. Once Ra'ouf completes dispensing the particulars of Saddam's expiration notice, he orders the condemned leader removed from court. Still protesting as he is led away, Saddam shouts his congratulations to the judge and the court. It shows a lack of camaraderie for Saddam to leave and not stick around for half-brother Barzon's verdict. It will be interesting to see Saddam's mood in a few days when the Anfal trial resumes. Until then, the "Tennyson of the Tigris" can write poetry.

By now Barzon knows he is not going to make that Caribbean cruise he promised his wife. He came into court yelling, then he sat politely during the verdicts, and now he has rediscovered his inner bratty child. Barzon's mood swings are one of his most endearing and entertaining qualities. But now the judge is imposing a new kind of swinging: The man who made callous complaints about his cigarette supply immediately following testimony about murdered families and destroyed farms, Barzon is receiving a special invitation to one of Iraq's most celebrated executions. The court isn't interested in hearing Barzon's displeasure with the death sentence, and his fifteen minutes are up.

Judge Ra'ouf immediately adjourns the court, the defendants are whisked away, and scheduled defendant statements are inexplicably omitted, probably out of fear that Barzon might attempt to filibuster his own execution. The reporters, long absent from any recent proceedings, rush from the court's viewing area down to the media room to spread the word. With a thirty-minute delay in our broadcast feed, we gather around the TV to watch our handiwork, listen to commentary, and take pictures.

As we watch the news catch up with the verdict, both CNN and Fox News are showing defendants and judges from the Anfal case, not the just-read Dujail trial verdict. Hey, what's the difference? Everybody is wearing robes and a funny scarf on their head; no one will notice. All of the American networks are predicting, almost hopefully, a surge in violence as the public reacts to the verdicts.

When we scan the channels for Arab news coverage we see people cheering and dancing in the streets in several cities. Iraq TV even discovers partying in radical cleric Muqtada al Sadr's Sadr City. Despite Baghdad's citywide curfew, it seems the entire populace is out to witness and celebrate this historic day for Iraq. Braving the evening curfew is a serious risk, since being caught outside means being shot on sight. But remember, these are the same people who defied the insurgency threats and stood in long lines to vote. Police and military patrols are probably not motivated to do much about enforcement violations tonight.

Switching back to the pessimistic side of news, American television is interviewing people "associated" with the trial. Not that we know everybody involved in the case, but no one in our cluster of attorneys, translators, and technicians has ever heard of these experts. Looking back at our monitors still showing the courtroom interior, the judges, aides, and prosecutors are all in court posing for group photos. There is a lot of smiling and handshaking.

The emboldened guards are in the defendants' cage proudly posing as well. On this day, the guards took control and did not succumb to intimidation by their former masters. I doubt the same warm and fuzzy feeling applies to the holding cells. I would love to know what is going on in that part of the building. Another translator comes in and tells us the judges have been hugging and crying in their chambers. One of them said, "The man who ruined our lives and country will now be punished." I double-checked the statement, and the judge was referring to Saddam, not President Bush.

As I exit the courthouse there is a wonderful excitement on the face of every Iraqi. The long-suffering people are relishing their liberation from the oppressive regime, and finally grasping that Saddam and his henchmen are not coming back. When I see my Iraqi friend Dr. K, he joyfully says that this is an historic day and Iraq is grateful. On behalf of Americans everywhere, I accept the praise. The normally stoic Iraqi guards wave, smile, and hug anyone within reach. This jubilation could only be eclipsed by an Iraq win in the World Cup.

Due to Baghdad's curfew the typical celebratory gunfire will likely be muted, and people will take their festivities inside, out of sight of Saddam loyalists and Sunni insurgents looking to make a headline. I expect Hussein's hometown of Tikrit will not be holding their weekly "Saddam look-alike" contest. As for me, I'm going to pass on going to the Red Zone for martinis and barbecue tonight.

To my delight, exuberant horn-honking and verdict celebrations resound across Baghdad for hours. From what I can hear across the river, my capricious Arabic translation is, "Damn the curfew, Saddam is going to hang." The next morning, honking cars driving through the Green Zone and across the Tigris signal the continuing Iraqi euphoria. There seems to be universal gratification in everyone's demeanor. It's like every person here feels they participated in some way to ending Saddam's reign of terror, and furthering Iraq's independence.

International reaction is more of a mixed bag. While many countries hail the conviction of Saddam Hussein, the death-penalty sentence garners little support. Reserving their enthusiasm is Great Britain, Australia, Canada, Italy, Russia, and numerous European countries. The only countries doing high-fives are the United States, Iraq and Kuwait. Both Amnesty International and Human Rights Watch condemn the trial procedure, the verdict, and the sentence; but then, those groups bitch about everything.

Conspiracy theorists, in between *Star Trek* conventions, are speculating about the verdict timing, relative to American midterm elections. Like the American government can tell the IHT and their judges what to do. Believe me, they tried to persuade the court numerous times, and the Iraqis didn't give a flying carpet.

It is just a matter of time before Human Rights Watch (HRW) issues a scathing report on Iraq. No, not on the indiscriminant bombing of innocents by the insurgency, but about rights violations during the Dujail trial and conviction of Saddam. These groups tend to focus more on the rights of murderers and terrorists, and ignore the multitudes being killed on their way to work, school, or markets. Do these groups ever criticize Hamas, Hezbollah, or al-Qaeda? Actually no, but they have defended Islamic extremists in

Uzbekistan, referring to them as "particularly pious." Uzbek Islamic scholars expelled HRW as "agitators."

Anyway, supposedly the HRW had an "observer" attend the entire trial. The group is claiming to furnish the "most comprehensive analysis to date." Well apparently, they did not consider the daily emails I sent to my wife. HRW further claims to have been in the courtroom several times. Oh really? That is not possible, unless their observer is one of the defense attorneys, a guard, or a judge. No one in the media or invited public could have witnessed the full story, because during sensitive testimony or belligerent arguments throughout the trial, the judge ordered the viewing-room curtains drawn numerous times, and observers were denied audio and video. While the feed to broadcast television was also halted, we continued making a video record of the proceedings. Besides, RCLO international law attorneys with impressive crimes-against-humanity credentials monitored the entire trial for irregularities and complications.

The HRW observer must have skipped the law class on brevity. The report is ninety-seven pages of redundant claims that Iraq ignored international law, failed to protect the defense attorneys and improperly replaced Judge Rizgar. There's more: the defense didn't get timely discovery; and the defendants couldn't confront witnesses.

What a load. It's true the IHT doesn't follow international law, *because the IHT is not an international court*. These trials are matters of state. Judge Rizgar was replaced because he didn't like criticism, and he was being run over by the defendants' political speeches. Time and again the defense attorneys made claims against the prosecution, only to be disproved as false manipulations. The defendants' insensitive questions to the witnesses were self-serving speeches that bordered on cruelty. And protecting the defense attorneys? The entire defense team declined U.S. protection and lodging several times. Maybe HRW is going to charge the defense lawyers weren't asked nicely enough.

There is no doubt the IHT fumbled and bumbled its way through Dujail. But this was the first trial of its type in a country enmeshed in a near civil war. Dujail was also the first televised trial in Iraq's history. It cannot be easy to have the world's microscope watching and criticizing every word and move. But the IHT did so many things right, and consider the opportunity it afforded the witnesses. The IHT had to convince witnesses to testify at the risk of loyalist retribution when they got home. After thirty-five years of tyranny, the IHT provided witnesses the chance to point at Saddam and his gang and say, "They did it."

But the HRW report says that's not important, that it's all about the flaws in Iraqi law. Look, without the RCLO here to guide this trial process, and the new Iraqi government wanting a legitimate trial, these old defendants would not have needed free medical care because there would have been public beheadings months ago. Now that would have made good television.

Within days of the HRW report, the IHT's final written decision is available. The document explains all the issues, and contradicts the HRW claims of injustice. That day I run into an Iraqi-American attorney from the RCLO. I have only heard brief accounts, but he has read the entire piece. He says the HRW report had so many falsehoods that the IHT written decision blows them away. He confidently says, "We Iraqis have our own laws. We don't care what they think."

He confides that when he confronted the HRW observer earlier, she denied even writing the report. He further explains that during the Dujail investigation, eighty-six people from the small farming village who cooperated with the inquiry were assassinated. Just this week, six people died the day after the HRW report was released. Unfortunately, the only story news organizations deem fit to report is the derisive HRW report.

Chapter 21

Back to Anfal

The air is filled with the sound of gunfire. Smoke blocks the sky and chokes the soldiers running to avoid the constant explosions and shrapnel that seem to be everywhere. Sand, sweat and fear are the only common denominators. When will this war end? It seems so black-and-white. Oh wait, that's the John Wayne movie I'm watching. It's time to get back to the Anfal trial, terrorism, the state of things here, and discussion about what colors are going to be hot this fall.

The first day in court after the Dujail verdicts is a somber one for the Anfal defendants. They file in slowly and quietly, seeming to comprehend this court means business, and that there will be no miraculous salvation for their evil deeds. Saddam spends most of the morning lost in his own thoughts, and writing. By the afternoon he puts on headphones so he can hear the Kurdish-to-Arabic translation during a video. Saddam seems out of sorts, like maybe he is catching a cold. He sneezes a lot. "Chemical" Ali and the other defendants respectfully ask their questions, and make no attempt at political statements. Perhaps the hangman's noose just added above the judges' bench is having an effect. Saddam even asks a polite question regarding one of his seventeen books introduced into evidence. I'm not sure what his books are about, but considering Saddam's penchant for poetry, perchance they are romantic prose.

But the newly transcendent Saddam can't help himself, and his relevant question becomes a metaphysical sermon as it veers off praising Allah, and asking Iraqis to forgive and get along. Well, that should about do it. Hugs everyone, this mess is cleared up. The troops and all of us can pack up and go home.

Kurdish witnesses captured by the army describe deaths, beatings and torture. Soldiers insert screwdrivers in open wounds to promote bleeding, and then douse the wound with an unknown yellow liquid to cause even more pain. Witnesses display dents in their heads from beatings, and scars on their backs from gunshots. A video is shown of a mass-grave excavation. The clothing remains, but there are no bodies, just bones. The skeletons are at rest inside the clothing and shoes, hats still cover skulls, and hand bones clutch prayer beads. Though the flesh has evaporated, the final agonizing struggles are captured in time. These people are speaking and bearing witness to the crimes and their terrifying last moments of life.

Each defendant asks witnesses for additional information regarding the atrocities. And since their original defense attorneys are still refusing to participate, the defendants ask the court for legal assistance. The defendants' cocksure days are over with the Dujail verdicts fresh on their minds. One attorney did show up earlier to accuse the prosecutor of withholding evidence. But like every other attorney before him, he was shown to be fabricating the charge. These defense attorneys need to develop a new scam to get delays. The new approach by the defendants, however, is showing some promise. They raised enough points with the judges to warrant a survey of an excavation site. None of the judges have yet seen any of the mass graves.

The defendants' theory is that the Iranians gassed the Kurds. There is no defense explanation for the Iraqi soldiers rounding up and shooting thousands of Kurds in cold blood, but that is just a messy detail. The defense theory makes no sense, because Saddam accused the Kurds of siding with Iran during the Iran-Iraq War. So as a thank-you, the Iranians gas their ally? Sounds logical. The Kurds hated, and still despise Saddam, and they aligned with the Kurds in Iran to keep both sides out of their region. There are also Kurds in Turkey who want to secede with the other Kurds and create an autonomous Kurdistan. The Kurdish ethnic group controls a large region rich in oil, and they are fiercely independent. But that's a whole other war yet to be fought.

The Kurdish fighters in the region are referred to as "Peshmerga," or "Those who face death." Peshmerga is a fun word to say, and all of us shout it out when it's mentioned. Our Kurdish attorney translators have even given us Kurdistan separatists' pins, but it's not really appropriate to wear them around an Iraqi government building. So, the judges are taking a road trip and that means another court break. Oh boy.

On the bright side, I have my own travel plans to make. Planning an exit strategy from this location and job requires patience and luck. First a replacement needs to found, preferably one that hasn't heard of Iraq, or seen the stories of escalating violence. Then the replacement needs to obtain travel clearance, which means they can't be wanted by the government. And they need to get final approval from their significant other to travel to a place where they could get killed. My wife is about to file "Crimes Against Marriage" charges on me if I don't come home soon.

And like the defendants here, I will not have a sound defense. My days of sleeping late, eating whenever I want, going to the gym, and enjoying a book are numbered.

The replacement's arrival will have to coincide with my departure, which will have to align with the screwy court schedule. And then there is that inconvenient armed action going on here to further complicate matters. I have to notify the military I am traveling, arrange for transportation out of Iraq, and request lodging. Hopefully my Kuwaiti seaside villa is available. And this all has to fit with a flight to anywhere out of the desert. It is a frustrating ballet of events as two people cross the globe, meet in Kuwait, and transfer the keys to Baghdad within a narrow window of opportunity.

I am eager to get out of here before someone gets rambunctious and hangs Saddam early. As of right now, the executions could happen any time in December. The lid is on pretty tight around insurgent violence at the moment, but the pressure is definitely building.

Tonight my coffee lounge is being taken over by the Marines. It is that time of year for the Marine Corps Ball, and for some reason I'm not invited. I consider approaching Ambassador Khalilzad about the invitation slight, but he looks busy with preparations. Though I let it go, for the life of me I can't imagine what kind of ball it will be since there are hardly any women here. I'm pretty sure I don't want the image of burly Marines "Gettin' Jiggy With It" stuck in my head, so I'm planning on watching some fine entertainment on Armed Forces Television.

I wake up the next day with a cold, or something sinus-related. It could be the Baghdad ambience, or a filthy trailer air filter that pumps out stuff that smells like an old camel. Before bed, I take some Extra Strength Tylenol that really sends me to another dimension. I nearly fall out of bed dreaming I am making a fast break in a basketball game. I don't play basketball. Anyway, I'm just glad there are no weapons in the trailer.

One of our crewmembers has to leave for a family emergency, so a replacement has arrived. He's a nice guy, but he loves to carry on long conversations, whether he gets a response or not. Since I sit and read in the Coffee Bean lounge most of the time, he has discovered a stationary target. After an hour of me saying, "Uh-huh" and not making eye contact, I give up and decide to leave. Why can't he just grunt and be unsocial like a normal man?

The discussion coming from several Washington talking heads about putting some of Iraq's burden on Syria and Iran has Iraqis nervous. To those weary of Operation Iraqi Freedom, this solution may seem logical and convenient, but it would put the proverbial fox in charge of the henhouse. Though Iran is Shi'a and Syria is a mixture, that doesn't mean the general population of Iraq likes either one of them. One Islamic sect doesn't always get along with others in the same sect. However they will unite if attacked by a common enemy. There is still great resentment amongst Iraqis toward Iran from the war over twenty years ago. Plus Iran is Persian not Arab, and they speak Farsi not Arabic.

Normally calm, peaceful Iraqis go ballistic when I bring up Iran. Even the Iraqi news uses "Iranians" to disrespectfully refer to Iraq's president and prime minister, who have ties to the despised Iran. Iraq's Sunnis don't want Iranian influence, which leaves neighboring Syria. Syria is a terrible neighbor, with its free-flowing borders of terrorism and contraband, and is only too happy exporting and protecting radicals while keeping an oppressive grip on its own population. Both Syria and Iran are complicit in keeping Iraq's insurgency funded and armed. It is in their interest to see Iraq struggle and democracy fail. The chaos elevates Iranian and Syrian regional prestige as mighty America fails and retreats. The Bush Administration seems to be confused and uninspired as it turns to countries labeled "terrorist states" for diplomatic assistance. I just wonder how puzzled our government will be when it comes to Iranian nuclear ambitions.

A large explosion rocked the embassy grounds yesterday, and today we found out the reason. We are located about a mile from the convention center where the Iraqi Parliament meets, across the street from the Al Rasheed Hotel. (The Al Rasheed is where CNN reporters watched the onslaught of Desert Storm.) During a parking-lot security sweep, bomb dogs detected something in two cars that caused them to signal an alert. An American demolition team blew up the cars, and two members of Parliament are currently without transportation. Because the men had government identification, earlier checkpoints didn't bother to examine them too closely. While the legislators aren't suspected of knowing their cars were wired, it shows how easy it is to transport bombs into the Green Zone. The Iraqi security status at entry checkpoints will now be increased from "Vulnerable" to "Mediocre."

The convention-center bomb is a real inconvenience. I was hoping to do some last-minute shopping at the Al Rasheed souvenir stores and pick up more Saddam pocket watches. They are a popular, economical gift item and only available at finer retailers, right next to the fake Rolex and Cartier watches. But traveling right now is not advised and requires a good reason. Sadly, the military does not consider shopping a good enough reason. There is a vendor's market in the Coffee Bean today, but it's mostly gaudy brass jewelry and overpriced rugs. The soldiers are eating this stuff up. Our little post office is going to enjoy transporting all those "authentic Persian" carpets made in India over to the States. And the girlfriends at home will really appreciate looking like tacky belly dancers.

It is Thanksgiving again and I can't believe this is the second one spent in Baghdad. While the year passed quickly, time has a funny way of dragging out an individual hour away from home. The DFAC is decked out with pilgrim mannequins and a titanic chocolate-cake Mayflower. The usual spread of high-caloric, artery-clogging food is just a reminder that none of us are home. After feeding my sorrows some turkey, and drowning my melancholy in mashed potatoes and gravy, I just wander around.

Traditional holidays create an unfathomable void when you find yourself truly alone. With a looming departure date just days away, I find my thoughts and emotions leaving this place. For most of my time so isolated, I push my emotions into a safe corner and just go about my routine keeping busy. But today, I catch myself in the transition of feeling, and there are still too many days to go to be this miserable. I have no choice but to read, sleep, watch television, and pretend the pain is not there. Since Iraq is eleven hours ahead of the States, football games won't be coming on for some time yet. Late into the night, soldiers will huddle around large-screen televisions brought in for the occasion, and for a few hours they will forget where they are. I know where I am, and I am homesick.

Another good reason to leave is that violence is escalating. The upswing could be a product of Saddam's verdict, tribal goat envy, or something worse. As I was moping around on Thanksgiving yesterday, all seemed quiet around the city. Boy, was I wrong. Government reports today say around two hundred people died, while people in the area claim around six hundred perished as a result of Sunni attacks. With the Middle East's love of exaggeration, it is hard to know the actuality.

According to my roommate Charles, friends of his in Sadr City said the militia was preparing to go out and eliminate all of the Sunnis in Baghdad. Apparently, the massacre was only stopped because U.S. forces sealed off the area. Besides Saddam's guilty verdict, the Sunnis can easily find justification for their attacks in other recent events. Iraq Prime Minister Nouri al-Maliki, a Shi'a and Muqtada al-Sadr buddy, has lately voiced a strong exclusionary statement that labels Sunni legislators as being obstructionists. Adding fuel to the embers, al-Sadr's Mahdi Army kidnapped some people from a Sunni education center last week, and yesterday was some symbolic day for Shi'a cleric Muqtada al-Sadr's deceased father. A government ministry building occupied by al-Sadr followers was attacked as well, and the siege ended when American helicopters showed up.

Part of the new Iraqi government's problem is the de-Ba'athification process that replaced qualified Sunni workers with Shi'a friends and uneducated militia members in ministry positions. The result is inefficiency, corruption, and attacks by thugs with official access, uniforms and vehicles. We hear all the time that "police" are breaking into homes and murdering people. It is not hard to believe, because military and police uniforms, hats, and armbands can be easily purchased from a street vendor. I should know, I bought some.

My doldrums have passed, and I'm now wearing a happy "I'm leaving and you're not" smile. My travel requests have come through, and I am booked at the Kuwait Hilton and Starbucks. There is, however, an apocalyptic note that states our government is closing the Federal Deployment Center (FDC), which is the acronym for Hilton's seaside villas, three weeks after my stay. Someone in Washington must have figured out how much the luxury accommodations were costing the taxpayers. While it's a bummer for the new guys coming through, I certainly don't want them to be deprived of the joys found in an Ali Al Salem desert tent.

But today it's a quick recheck of court equipment, and we feel prepared for the next few sessions of the trial. The court expects to conclude testimony in the Anfal case during my final days, and I will bid a fond and ultimate farewell to Saddam.

The Anfal court is finally ready to resume with all the drama, forensics, and incompetence we have come to expect. It almost makes me want to stay for the rest of the trials. Not really. Just as court is scheduled to begin, and seeing how the Iraqi judges love a good delay, they actually vote and arrive at a 3-2 decision to break for tea. Since I have my own coffee pot, I wholeheartedly approve of the vote. For once, there is a good reason for this break. Because of the weekend insurgency activity there is an inclusive curfew, which means roads and the airport are closed.

The defense attorneys, who insist on living outside the safety of the Green Zone, are having problems traveling, because they are essentially defying the curfew. The attorneys are already in danger of being killed by Shi'a militias; now they are facing the U.S. military. But considering the testimony the defense is about to hear, perhaps an ambush would be preferable.

Once everyone has a nice caffeine buzz, and the defense attorneys talk their way through checkpoints, we are ready to begin. Unless someone on the court staff decides it's time for lunch. Defense attorney Badie Arif Azzat, dubbed the "Carpet Salesman" by the control room, is rather chubby, has atrocious fashion sense, and is dreadfully smarmy. He begins the day anew by arguing with Judge Mohammed about defense witnesses. Badie claims his team is having trouble getting people to willingly testify on behalf of Saddam Hussein.

In a mind-blowing revelation, the potential defense witnesses fear association with their former leader, or being arrested. Of course, pleads Badie, a delay will help the situation. You know, I could swear I heard this argument about a month ago, and as it turns out, I did.

The judge already gave the defense a twenty-day extension, then added two more days to the pot.

"But your honor," the desperate cherub implores, "some have fled the country, or changed their identity. How are we to find them?"

If I were one of Saddam's cohorts, I would have jumped on the first caravan out of town too. At this point, the defendants realize in the last month, little or nothing has been done to help their case. The accused rightfully leap to their feet and voice displeasure. The judge isn't swayed or impressed, and calls for the day's first witness. In other words, "Hey, you're getting what you paid for, boys. Now sit down."

The first few Kurdish witnesses provide gruesome detail to the killing along the newly dug trenches. As the bullets start to fly they see family members shot, they hear their screams, and watch heads blowing apart. Even in translation the story maintains its sense of horror and helplessness. Over and over, so many have the same details to share, and each witness is standing up for the loved ones they still mourn. I understand why it needs to be said and yet, the stories become numbing.

Despite the repetition, the prosecution claims this testimony is just a fraction of the 180,000 potential stories of death during the Anfal Campaign. While witnesses on the stand cry for their lost children, Saddam closes his eyes and turns his back on them to begin a hyperbolic façade of prayer to a higher power. When Saddam concludes his demonstration of faith, the prayer goes unanswered; he remains on trial and he is still not president. Though Hussein turns to face the front, he is about to face the music.

If there had been any doubt about the truthfulness regarding the terrors experienced by the Kurdish survivors and victims, the prosecution's forensic experts quash any reasonable concerns. When the first forensic anthropologist expert is introduced to the court, the defense immediately objects. The attorneys argue they do not have a witness of equivalent qualifications to refute him. They whine, "How will we know what to ask?" Obviously, this evidence is going to be really bad for their clients, and there is no credible defense against it.

The defense acts like the impending testimony is a big Perry Mason moment being sprung on them by surprise. They actually would like the judge to just make it go away. In so many words the judge replies, "Nope, but thanks for asking." Finally, there are going to be English-speaking witnesses I can understand.

American forensic expert Dr. Clyde Snow, who researched a mass gravesite in northern Iraq in the early 1990s, testifies to the murder of almost thirty men and adolescent boys from the Kurdish town of Koreme. The bodies, wearing traditional Kurdish clothing, were unearthed in a grave. Saddam implies in his questioning of Dr. Snow that the discovered bodies might have been moved and placed as some sort of conspiracy. Oh yes, that is a great theory. Picture the scenario of disappointed forensic scientists concocting some evil scheme when they discover a mass grave doesn't contain enough dead Kurds, so the archaeologists devise a plan to truck in more bodies from a different massacre site to make it look better. It's that kind of out-of-the-box thinking that made Saddam president.

Another doctor testifies about observing the effects of chemical weapons on Kurdish refugees in 1988. Through soil samples and patient examinations, he detects traces of the nerve agent sarin, and a mustard gas similar in composition to that employed by the Nazis. These two witnesses not only establish the manners of death while the graves are relatively "fresh" and the use of outlawed chemical weapons, but they also point to the selective ethnicity of the victims.

Explaining ballistic evidence from the same site as Dr. Snow, archaeology expert Douglass Scott details the shooting pattern of the Iraqi soldiers. Though the defendants seem entranced by what can be discovered forensically, they are probably wishing they had covered their tracks better. Using diagrams and locations of bullet casings, Scott is able to pinpoint where shooters stood, and the horizontal pattern they used in gunning down the hapless victims. Scott could follow specific gunmen as they walked around firing into the death pit. With little regard or concern to hide their crime, soldiers left ejected casings right where they dropped from the Kalashnikov automatic rifles.

During cross-examination, the "Carpet Salesman," Badie Arif Azzat, keeps asking the same rudimentary questions as if he is just not able to comprehend how forensic science works. Frustrated, he refers to Prosecutor Munqidh and the judges as "brother," and complains to the court the evidence is just too complicated. (Not to mention incredibly damaging.) By addressing the judges as "brother" instead of their proper title, a shouting match ensues between Badie and Judge Mohammed.

These Iraqi judges react in odd ways. Defense attorneys or defendants can derisively say something I think is going to set off hostilities, and nothing happens. Then when an expression as superficially innocuous as "brother" is mentioned, all hell breaks loose. It must be a cultural phenomenon. Insulted and out of patience, Judge Mohammed ejects the "Carpet Salesman." The chubby attorney is whisked away by guards, kicking and screaming all the way out the door.

Ironically, Badie has been occupying the same seat formerly used by Ramsey Clark. That chair has some bad karma. The attorney is arrested outside the door and camera view, and taken to an Iraqi jail. Badie will have a fun time behind bars once inmates find out he's defending Saddam. Despite pleas and apologies from the defendants and defense counsel, the judge lets the attorney sit in jail all day.

The last expert witness for the prosecution in the Anfal case is riveting beyond expectations. From the Army Corps of Engineers comes the internationally recognized authority in forensic archaeology in charge of the Mass Graves Project. Dr. Michael "Sonny" Trimble is responsible for the last several years of investigations that scientifically examined the mass graves strewn about Iraq. For long periods, Dr. Trimble and his team braved the environment and insurgency harassment in areas not controlled by Coalition forces. To stay safe and to complete their task, the scientists worked long hours, and were often confined to small encampments surrounded by a security detail.

But the information gleaned from their work is phenomenal and gut-wrenching. Using the large map looming on the wall beside the judges, Dr. Trimble describes the various locations and excavations. I'm sure the defense is going to object to the omnipresent map: "Where did that come from?"

In evidence that should lead the evening news, but won't, Dr. Trimble details his findings at a site dig called Muthanna 2. Perhaps because of earlier language barriers, to me this testimony takes all of us into these Kurds' ill-fated final moments like no witness before. The Muthanna 2 site contained ten shallow graves that were only dug about knee depth because of difficult bedrock. (The soldiers probably thought that there was no need go to too much trouble for a mass killing. No one is ever going to look for these people.) At Muthanna 2, one hundred and fourteen bodies were discovered—two males, twenty-seven females, and eighty-five children. Since the defendants claim to only have targeted instigators, this grave must have held the heart of the peshmerga revolt against Saddam. For some reason at this juncture, Prosecutor Munqidh rubs his teeth and smells his finger.

Now Dr. Trimble gets down to the macabre details of his discovery, complete with photographic evidence. This will be as difficult to read as it is agonizing to recall. A girl around the age of five or six is shot in the torso and legs; her femur is blown in half, and her feet still have on Top Cat boots. Another girl, age eight or ten, has multiple wounds in the torso and head. Her rotated head and wounds indicate she was trying to escape the incoming fire. Despite her efforts she is shot in the eye, jaw, and her spine. A near-term pregnant female, holding an older child in front of her, is shot through the stomach. One deadly bullet kills a mother, daughter, and unborn child.

Saddam brazenly yawns.

A child no older than three to nine months shows damaged ribs from his mother falling on him. The mother dies still holding her son tightly, the baby likely suffocating from the carnage or buried alive. A female in her late teens or early twenties is shot at least ten times. A woman around the same age is shot through the hands and arms as she twists away from the bullets. Her head explodes apart.

In all, the average adult is shot nine times; children an average of four shots each. Sixty-one percent of the victims found in the Muthanna 2 grave are children.

Trimble's presentation highlights only a selected, representative group of victims from the site. As he speaks of each person, a screen displays how the body was found, then the skeleton, and followed by recovered personal items. Then Trimble, using a mannequin approximately the size of the victim, shows the victim's clothing placed on the inanimate figurine. The images of women's brightly colored, bullet-ridden clothes draped in jewelry are haunting. Some mannequins clutch the swaddled specter of murdered infants to their breasts. Some of the victims die holding treasured possessions like perfume, baby items, and toys. Some mannequins are bound or blindfolded. Many of the female victims hid and retained their identification by sewing them into their clothes.

Due to Islamic protocol, the Muslim male soldiers did not thoroughly hand-search the women for papers. With all the savagery and degradation, a final act of religious etiquette by the soldiers allows the investigators to place a name and a face to certain victims. Never forgotten by their families, these vulnerable missing souls who perished so violently, long ago discarded in a heap and buried, are finally having their say. After being lost ghosts for twenty years, they have returned to make sure Saddam and his thugs don't forget them either. The testimony and presentation is not lost on the judges as several dab their eyes.

Trimble moves on to another site called Ninawa 2. This scene is equally as grisly with the discovery of one hundred and twenty-three bodies. Evidence points to soldiers leading the victims in two groups into the trench. The first group is shot singly in the head, while standing or kneeling. The second group either falls or is dumped on top of the first victims. The doctor's team finds a fetus skeleton within the mother, who was shot in the back of the head, expelling her face. Trimble displays both the mother and the unborn infant's skeletons, along with the woman's sweater, dress, and scarf. Inside her clothing, a photo ID is found and shown to the court. Her face forever frozen in time, she bears witness today.

A child between six and twelve months old is found shot in the back of the head. Witnessing her baby's murder, the mother's hand still clutches the deceased baby and its blanket as she too is shot in the head. A girl between seven and twelve is shot in the head as she holds a plastic bowl. Twenty-five of the recovered corpses at Ninawa 2 are women, and the remaining ninety-eight bodies are children. Nearly 90 percent of the children slaughtered at this site are less than thirteen years of age. Many of the dead have no gunshot wounds, indicating they died after burial.

Ninawa 9 is an ambitious ten-feet-deep wedge-like grave. Trimble's team reconstructs a scene in which sixty-four Kurdish males are herded into the pit.

Standing atop the edge of the trench, Saddam's soldiers begin firing at the legs of the captives to prevent them from running. As the fire rains down upon them, many of the victim's heads burst apart. Dr. Trimble says that bullet casings litter the area all around the pit where the soldiers sprayed fire into their prey.

Saddam again yawns, and then turns in his chair to face away from the witness. This motion is not out of revulsion, but disdain for the proceedings, and a need to offer his prayers once again for the benefit of the viewing public.

Iraqi law allows the defendants to cross-examine the witness, but in this instance the judge is requiring the questions be directed to him, and he will then inquire the witness. This judicial filter might be a good mechanism to prevent the defendants from fermenting confusion with political statements, and encourage them to focus instead on actually clarifying evidential matters. With such damning testimony before them, all of the defendants should take the opportunity to participate.

The defense attorneys first suggest that the bodies found were just collateral victims from the Iraq-Iran War, but the effort is half-hearted at best. Even the delusional defense team can't believe that theory. One by one the defendants get up to question Trimble about any evidence found on the victims that implicates them personally. They also doubt the reliability of Trimble's manner of death findings. While none of the victims bore a handy death notice attached to them, and the site did not have a large marker placed above the grave stating, Kurds buried here because they needed killin', the prosecution has plenty of signed documents fitting the bill. Much like Dujail, the defendants will deny it is their signature affixed to incriminating regime papers. As to manner of death, it doesn't take much of a Hippocratic deduction to figure that one out.

A perplexed "Chemical" Ali isn't too sure the mass graves are even in Iraq, because maybe they are "somewhere else." We know, Ali, there's a lot of desert in these parts. But, if anybody should know, it would be you, Ali, the monster that orchestrated the genocide. The fabricated sincerity and impudence shown by these bastards is deplorable.

Saddam, freshly revitalized from his spiritual reflection, rises and begins with a prayer, "In the name of God"… blah, blah… "Let us die as Muslims." (I whimsically expect the judges to give thumbs-up at this convenient offer.) Returning from his thoughts of paradise, Saddam wonders how the trial moved to mass graves; he believed the trial was about the "military" campaign of Anfal.

"It all seems to be convoluted and moving so quickly. Is the court in a hurry?" Saddam asks. After spending the last several hours experiencing the atrocities, Judge Mohammed smacks the former president with "If you paid attention" you would know how these graves relate to Anfal. Undeterred and calm, Saddam asks that an impartial expert be brought in and examine the graves. I think maybe Saddam is going for any kind of delay at this point.

Saddam states he doesn't trust any American experts. "Well, that's just too bad," replies Judge Mohammed.

As the defendant questions get repetitive and without purpose, except to extol their innocence, Judge Mohammed calls a halt to the gum-flapping.

Notwithstanding objections from the defense, and defendant "Chemical" Ali who states, "I have every right to defend myself, unless the court wants to deprive me of my rights. Then I will trouble the court no further." In a normal court that might and should work, but after these appalling images and descriptions, everyone has had enough of the defendants' self-serving lies.

There are still tens of thousands, perhaps even ten times that number of Kurds still unaccounted for and buried in the vast, lonely deserts of Iraq. Dr. Trimble and the Mass Graves Project detailed only three sites out of the two hundred graves known to exist. There are no resources to fully excavate and reclaim the innocent victims who will be forever lost. Once the American team leaves, Iraq will not have the motivation, or the Kurds the technology, to return the missing to their families.

At the conclusion of Dr. Trimble's moving testimony and presentation, Judge Mohammed adjourns the court. I have just witnessed and participated in my last day of the trials of Saddam Hussein.

Chapter 22

Time To Say Goodbye

Exhaustion, sadness, relief, anticipation: I have so many feelings right now. The testimony of Dr. Trimble is something I'll never forget. It's like I just witnessed a day at the Nuremburg trials that detailed Nazi death camps and atrocities of the Holocaust. How can people treat other humans this way, and go on living as if they have done nothing wrong? How can they justify the actions, and even deny what sights and sounds they witnessed? What goes through the minds of the Iraqi soldiers who participated in Anfal as their own children grow up, and perhaps succumb to sectarian violence?

This view of the world is too depressing. I look forward to going home and just worrying about something trivial like my impending jury summons.

The time to pack for my journey is upon me, and despite not getting all the souvenirs I wanted, there is still too much to fit in my luggage. The PX has inexpensive footlockers that can hold quite a stash, so I grab one and take it back to the trailer. The locker is easy enough to carry empty. After loading the locker up with all my new goodies, I suddenly have more than enough room for extra junk. With space, cash, and time, that means shopping. There is group of local vendors next to the bombed-out Republican Guard headquarters down the way that feed off people like me, so I head over there. There are the predictable rugs, and exquisite paintings of seductive Arabic women draped over a lion, or riding a stallion.

And there are recent bootleg movies for a dollar or two. I bought a Harry Potter movie earlier. The quality was pretty good until about halfway through, when silhouettes of people getting up and going to get popcorn walked through the frame.

Winding back through an electronics store, that becomes an Internet café, which becomes storage, the hall leads me to an antique store. Thank goodness I didn't find this place earlier, or my trailer would have looked like the interior of Barbara Eden's bottle. In one corner are historical photos of streets lined with camels and palm trees during Baghdad's glory days. In other corners sit Arabic radios, product canisters, English pith helmets, knives and swords, all from the '30s era. Helmets and uniforms from the Iraq-Iran War era are too creepy. I'm thinking they could be Anfal-related. Dozens of military medals from forgotten soldiers cover a section of wall.

Nestled in the collection are numerous swastika badges from Iraq's brief World War II Nazi era. These are the real deal and historically fascinating, but I can't imagine having something that offensive in my possession going through Immigration, and my wife would kill me, so I pass. Then I find what I want. It is way overpriced. But I rationalize that I won't be here again.

A few months ago I went to a store near the court looking for some unique souvenirs. Unfortunately, the shop was located in the same apartment complex where courthouse security suspected that people were planning an attack against trial participants. Security then put up a large screen to block both the view and rocket-propelled grenades. This area is probably not the best place to go, but who doesn't like a little danger when bargain-hunting?

Anyway, I came across a thick silver medallion, like a giant coin, with Saddam's portrait on one side, and a green inlaid map of some type on the reverse. It was pretty worn, but I didn't want the shop owner to shoot me, so I bought it. I had no idea what it was. Now, before me are the medallions in silver or bronze, in mint condition with the original boxes. Even better the salesman knows what they are. They are commemorative medallions issued for Saddam's first anniversary of being president in 1980. The medallions were given as gifts to prestigious loyal followers, and dominantly displayed in homes. The salesman tells me the medallion acted as a "Stay out of jail" card. Someone likely carried my worn medallion around for protection.

These days, I think the aura has worn off the magic medallion. The countries on the back of the medallion represent Arabic lands, from Iraq to Saudi Arabia and around the top of Africa. The map is like one of those weird pictures with a dinosaur hidden in the squiggly image. Once somebody points it out, the figure is obvious. Under Saddam's portrait are the words "The President, Leader, Struggler, Saddam Hussein."

Once light when filled with air, my footlocker is now jammed with books, clothes, and enough souvenirs to open my own "Little Baghdad" shop when I get home. Having too much free time and a credit card is a terrible combination. Especially when the only thing to buy is junk. Am I really going to wear that t-shirt with "Stay back 200 feet or you will be shot" emblazoned on the back, in Arabic? Well, I have two versions in case I do. And then there are those small colorful rugs I bought as floor mats until I found out they were Islamic prayer rugs. And those miniature statues from Mesopotamia's history are going to look really nice stuck in a closet. And then there are all those editions of *Stars and Stripes* I'm keeping. I started out just saving the "significant news" issues, but when nearly every day in the war is significant ... well, okay, I'm a hoarder.

Then I get to drag my box of treasures all the way to the post office and get it cleared. By the time I get there I am radiating a beautiful glow. The customs inspector probably either thinks I am nervous about the contents, or ready for an angioplasty. The inspectors are young military personnel lucky enough to get an office job instead of poking out of a patrolling Humvee. They completely unpack and search the footlocker for contraband. We can't mail explosives, guns, or any of Saddam's swords. This is Iraq however, so gold bullion and large stacks of American cash are okay.

I am being beckoned to the RCLO office, and hopefully it doesn't mean the warden is canceling my parole. Instead, the military attaché presents a certificate of appreciation for my contributions, and a ceremonial Iraqi flag that flew over the courthouse on my last day of trial. This flag will serve as a symbolic and emotional reminder of not only my time here, but the historic testimony and bravery of the Kurds. It is also time to say goodbye to my Iraqi friends. I ordered some books online a month ago to give my mentor Dr. K, in gratitude for all he has taught me. Current reading material is a precious commodity over here for the Iraqis; it's expensive and hard to find. My friend is touched and grateful.

The Iraqis are so moved by small expressions of consideration, from offered bottles of water to a few selected books. It just seems we could do so much better over here listening to Iraqis' basic needs, rather than telling them all the grand things they should have. My friends proudly pose for several pictures around the embassy until security approaches me: "You know you aren't supposed to photograph in here. I'm going to have to report you." Sure, like I care, I'm leaving tonight. Somewhere in the embassy system I have a demerit and an unfulfilled detention in the ambassador's office.

One last meal at the DFAC, and sadly one last soft-serve chocolate ice cream cone. A final stroll through the halls of the embassy amongst the soldiers and civilians moving from one place to another reveals that life will go on without me. Everyday people come and go. Some are lounging in the Coffee Bean; some are just trying to find their bearings. Some of the people volunteered to come here, but most didn't. I am the lucky one, because I am leaving. There are still several hours before tonight's Rhino run, so I hang out in the lounge. This place is so familiar I can't imagine how I could have occupied my time without it.

When I first arrived this was a large empty room. Slowly furniture arrived, then computers, then a help desk, and finally rows of books and magazines. Reading, writing, drinking coffee, talking with friends, and people watching kept me sane and entertained. But tonight I see it for what it is. Around me is the laughter and conversation of people trying to make the best of an adverse, lonely situation. The guys at the coffee counter are playing the same music CD they play on most nights. They have it for sale, so I buy one. I am anxious to see if the music transports me back to Iraq every time I hear it.

Now it is time to head to the Rhino where I can sign in and wait. A process that used to incite anxiety is now just a necessary step to get home. I leave feeling a real pride in my role here, of taking a risk, and witnessing history. Waiting to load, I'm taking in all of my last looks. The Republican Palace is really quite beautiful, even at one in the morning. The row of Rhinos still look like fortified Winnebagos ready for some extreme camping. And I still look like a complete geek wearing a helmet and my body armor.

I climb aboard the Rhino and take a window seat. There will be no sleeping on this ride, because I don't want to miss anything. We go through the dark city, into the residential areas, and stop once again at the isolated, amber-lit checkpoint on Route Irish. You push out of your mind that a wheel might hit an IED, or at any moment an attack could occur. This is the life of the marshals, drivers, and military escort who ferry back and forth, twice a night, every day.

We arrive at the Rhino "Stables" at Camp Victory and unload. Tonight, I am fortunate to get transferred over to temporary housing next to the airport where I can sleep in a bed. I feel for the guys stuck here all night in the hot, stuffy air playing cards and watching television. Check-in at the military version of Motel 6 goes smoothly. The group of new temporary buildings is clean and well lit, with quaint landscape touches behind a security fence. The shared rooms have several beds, but I seem to be the only one around. I doubt anyone else will be coming tonight, since it's about four in the morning.

After a few hours' nap, I hit a small PX for packaged donuts and coffee. Traveling can be harsh, and I need to keep up my strength. It's a short walk to the building to catch the lumbering C-130. The same guys are instructing people on how to walk in a straight line over the tarmac towards the plane. That's a job with a future. Across the runway is the terminal where I first arrived a year ago. It doesn't seem that long ago that a bunch of us loaded into Humvees accidentally bound for Route Irish.

Before boarding I turn and bid farewell to Iraq. I will miss my friends and forever remember them, but I am damn glad to be getting out while the getting is good. I am such a seasoned veteran of these transport flights that I quickly fall asleep and don't wake until Kuwait. Exhaustion can be your friend.

Before I board the bus that takes me to the Kuwait Hilton late that night, I pass more construction on the American side of the Ali al Salem base. Even more military vehicles and supplies sit poised to go somewhere. It doesn't appear the United States has any intention of leaving anytime soon. After twelve hours of hanging around the sand and tacky shops at the base, I board the midnight bus to the Hilton villas. My flight home doesn't leave until the following night, so tomorrow I can enjoy all that Kuwait City has to offer.

I wake thirteen hours later. So much for sightseeing, but there is a Starbucks with my name on it. With the temperature at 100-plus degrees outside, the Hilton's Starbucks is a perfect, intimate world.

Flying from Kuwait City to Amsterdam is a snooze. It's a long flight, and I'm out of the desert, but there is still a long way to go. Some of our television crew that went through this way stopped to do some sightseeing, but right now the glories of Europe are not alluring. Once my plane crosses over the North Atlantic's retreating ice caps, and the fished out waters of Nova Scotia, I spot the shores of home and start humming "Star-Spangled Banner."

Next stop is Washington D.C., the city with a higher mortality rate than Iraq. While touching down on American soil presents such a sense of tranquility, that euphoria is short-lived as soon as I get stuck in customs security. Can't they just devise two lines, one for people with evil intent, and the other for people just wanting to get home? The customs official is not at all impressed with where I just came from, my Department of Defense identification, or passport littered with Middle East stamps. He is more suspicious about why I have a heavy, ceramic-plated flak vest. Perhaps by putting on the helmet and opening myself to ridicule, he'll see I am not a threat to national security.

After showing the appropriate authorizing letters, I am finally through the inquisition and sprinting to my connection gate, which is of course on the other side of the airport. After coming this far, missing a flight is not an option. While waiting to board some people are looking at me, and then one comes up and says gratefully, "Thank you for your service." I thank them politely, but let them know I am not a soldier. No, I am not wearing my helmet; I am, however, toting a camouflaged Army backpack from the PX. Coupled with my chiseled physique, it's an honest mistake.

In a few hours I am walking through my home terminal, and upon reaching the escalators I see my wife waiting below. She looks wonderful. This has been a hard trip for her, hearing reports about bombings and violence, and not being able to ask or be told what is happening. After the blur of traveling halfway around the world, I am in a daze from all the activity around me. I have just arrived from a country at war, working on a trial everyone knows about, and yet I am not unique around baggage claim. Other people with their own stories are arriving and meeting their loved ones, but none are as happy as me.

Home is eerily quiet without generators, helicopters, or the heart-stopping thud of mortars. This is a different world without the fear of animosity and imminent danger. It's as if the ugliness in life doesn't exist here. I spend the next few weeks reacquainting myself with our culture of freedom, and enjoying the independence of moving about without trepidation, or an armed driver.

The Anfal trial continues back in Baghdad with the introduction of document evidence. It comes as no surprise to hear that Saddam is acting up and wants to be excused. Saddam's Dujail conviction is going through an appeals process that will be a rubber stamp for death. But the trial receives little more than a passing reference in the news. The insurgency violence that is rapidly escalating dominates the coverage. Unless there is footage of a bombed-out market and scattered bodies, no one seemingly cares.

After missing last Christmas at home, the whole family gets together, and for better or worse, everyone is the recipient of Baghdad embassy attire. I am busy enjoying the holidays getting reacquainted with family and alcohol, and not paying attention to the news.

While emerging for a coffee run, I see a newspaper headline. Saddam has been executed.

My first thought is how fortunate I am for leaving before it happened, but then my thoughts turn to what kind of response my Baghdad co-workers might suffer. Surely there will be celebrating, but radicals may use the event as an excuse to get excited too. Some months ago, an Iraqi lawmaker suggested hanging Saddam at the Swords of Victory monument within the Green Zone, complete with bleachers and lights. As a pay-per-view event, the idea might have been brilliant.

But thinking back, prior to the trials when we first went to Iraq, there was serious discussion about videotaping the executions. My morbid curiosity and naiveté made it seem like a good idea. Thank goodness wiser heads prevailed and we weren't assigned to record the hanging for the world. At the time however, I don't think anyone anticipated or considered the temptation of our digital age.

The world is shocked to learn someone in fact illicitly records the execution, in all its brutality and savagery on a smuggled cellphone camera. The video of a defiant Saddam and angry, barbaric guards streaks across the Internet, and justly reinforces the perception of a sham trial and execution based on sectarian vengeance. While the cellphone audio is mostly imperceptible, one of the voices demanding calm and dignity is Prosecutor Munqidh. Lost in the horror of the hanging is the Iraqi law that allows, and actually requires, execution within thirty days of the conviction being upheld.

As wrong as it seems to the general public, Saddam is given just three days.

While Iraq and Texas may be used to rapid death sentences, the rest of the world is not. There is universal condemnation for the execution, but at least Americans had nothing to do with carrying out the sentence.

Saddam had been transferred into Iraqi hands at the request of Prime Minister Maliki, and removed from American protection. He was taken to an Iraqi intelligence base in Baghdad. It was a shame really that Saddam be executed in such a wrathful manner. The hasty and secretive removal of Saddam denied the Kurds their justice.

Once Saddam was hanged, charges against him were dropped for the crimes of Anfal. Saddam's death also prevented him from facing the accusers of the upcoming Marsh Arab trial. Though Saddam could only be executed once, he should have had to endure his atrocities and convictions in court. The rationale of the Iraqi government was to try and quickly heal the country, and to remove Hussein as a lightning rod for the insurgency. But the greater insurgency did not rally around Saddam or his Ba'athist regime.

The pre-dawn execution was also meant to avoid the weeklong ban on executions due to begin at sun up for the religious Eid al-Adha festival. Timing is everything.

Only Saddam's hometown of Tikrit, where he was buried, showed initial signs of anger and revenge, and even that outrage faded. The rumors of Hussein fleeing the country, or having one of his doubles executed, was just speculation from untrusting Arab imaginations. It was not unreasonable to doubt the execution, because Iraqis had seen Saddam defy the world's mightiest military power, evade precision bombs, and escape death from numerous assassination attempts for decades.

The skeptical Iraqi public demanded photographic proof in the earlier deaths of Saddam's sons Uday and Qusay, and terrorist Al Zarqawi. In the end, because of a gruesome video that repulsed the world, the population of Iraq became convinced Saddam was gone and never returning.

Three weeks later Saddam's irascible half brother Barzon is hanged along with "Dr. Evil" Awad Bandar, the former head of the Revolutionary Court. In a fitting finale, Barzon loses his head during the execution. Taha Ramadan, the mousy former vice-president originally sentenced to life imprisonment, is hanged three months later. His sentence is likely enhanced because of his proclivity for picking his nose on camera.

For the crimes at Anfal, in June 2007, charges against Tahir Tawfiq al-Aani are dropped; Farhan Mutlaq al-Jabouri and Sabir Abd al-Aziz al-Douri receive multiple life sentences; while Sultan Hashem Ahmed al-Ta'i, Husayn Rashid al-Tikriti, and Saddam's cousin "Chemical" Ali Hassan al-Majid al-Tikriti receive death sentences.

"Chemical" Ali is hanged on January 25, 2010. Tariq Aziz is convicted in two trials and sentenced to long terms in prison. An Iraqi judicial review later changes Aziz's sentence to death, but President Talibani never approves the execution order.

The Regime Crimes Liaison's Office television coverage of the Anfal case, and defendant "Chemical"

Ali's trial for his role in suppressing a Shi'a uprising, continues into 2008. Ultimately, after Saddam's death there seems little public interest or propaganda benefit to warrant further American taxpayer expense for worldwide broadcasting from the Iraqi High Tribunal.

Iraqi state-run television and the IHT take over the responsibility of providing subsequent trial coverage. With the mission complete, our crew retrieves hundreds of boxes from the bombed-out upper floor and shakes off the dust and rat droppings. They carefully repack the delicate equipment that recorded history for a long trip back home.

After more than two years of covering the "Mother of All Trials," the lights are turned off and the door is closed.

Afterward

An Incomplete, Abridged, Generalized History of the Arab Conflict.

During breaks in the trial I wanted to further explore and understand the history and rationale of the Middle East, and why the Islamic world feels like the Western world is against them. After reading works of renowned Middle East authority Bernard Lewis and others, and researching historical websites, I composed a condensed version of events that created this conflict. (Remember, there's a lot of spare time during this trial.)

As far as I can tell, the history of mankind's actions comes down to two distinct factors: religion and economics. One is not dependent on the other, but they work more effectively together. Both have caused well-documented destruction of civilizations and cultures. Religion has been often used as an excuse for greed and the pursuit of power. Economic domination has imposed new doctrines and forbidden established beliefs. The common method of establishing these new ideas and opportunities has been slaughtering the disadvantaged and conquered population into submission. Having control of one usually brought the command of the other.

To somewhat understand Islamic extremism, the passion of hate and why it exists, we have to go back in time. We also have to think less like Westerners and more like Islamic fundamentalists—which is to say in effect, throw all rationales out the window.

Long, long ago, a child was about to be born. The mother had a premonition of lights, and she received a name. The child arrived and he exhibited many signs

239

and wonders. His given name meant "The Glorified," but his friends just called him Muhammad. The year was 570 A.D. and the city was Mecca. Religions at the time in this desolate tribal culture were based on varied pagan worship. Christianity and Judaism did not tempt the Arab. For the next forty years, Muhammad reveled in the good life, surrounded by herds of goats and date palms. He led a fairly uneventful existence, except for an earlier time when angels pulled out his heart, and put snow on it to cleanse it, which is why Muslims wash before prayers.

But, then Muhammad experienced the "Night Journey," and life on this planet would change forever.

During the "Night Journey," Muhammad was taken by the angel Gabriel to Jerusalem's Temple Mount, and introduced to Abraham, Moses, and Jesus. He was shown that he was the Prophet that would rescue and redeem faith in the one true God. After the journey, Muhammad withdrew to a cave where he received revelations and verses from Gabriel. In the "Recitation" or Qur'an, the previously illiterate Muhammad recorded his experiences, and shared them with immediate family and friends. The original believers were called "Companions" and are still revered in Islam.

As the belief spread and gained popularity, it also gained the attention of the pagan sects. These new ideas of one God and law were rejected by the idol worshipers in Mecca, and seen as a threat to clan and tribal authority. To escape their wrath, Muhammad and his followers fled to nearby Yathrib, later known as Medina, "City of the Prophet." Over time, the new faith gained immense acceptance and many followed.

The "Sirah," or life of Muhammad, and the "Hadith," the oral communications and teachings of the Qur'an, make up the "Sunna," the example or usage, from which faith, morals, and doctrine are based. (And from which "Sunni" is derived.) Traditional Islam is based on compassion and defined laws. To Muhammad, all religions and people were equals in peace, but God did not negotiate. Islam recognizes four books: the Qur'an, Torah, Psalms of David, and the Gospels.

The Gospels are important to the Muslims and are respected, and Jesus is considered a Prophet. Muhammad even traced his ancestry back to Ishmael, one of Abraham's sons. But "People of the Book," Christians and Jews, only have part of the story. To Muslims, all other religions are either false, or incomplete. The final revelation and truth is the Qur'an. These three distinct faiths, Islam, Christianity and Judaism, are just branches from the same religious origin.

While the Qur'an has some fiery passages that radicals have taken out of context for self-serving reasons, it contains more words of tolerance. It includes some stories, but reads more like graceful, lyrical verses. "Hallaj" means God alone decides which faith people choose, and there should be no conflict between them. It commands followers to respect and honor those of the Torah and Gospels as long as there is a belief in the one God. As with many passages within the Qur'an, extremists skim over inconvenient messages of understanding, such as God saying to the Israelites, "Dwell in this land."

Apocalyptic phrases appear as a warning to anyone who makes war on Islam, or drives believers from their homes. But calls for aggression are in retribution only. Even those captured in battle are allowed to pass unharmed if they profess their belief in God. Those that don't are "Unbelievers" and should die (i.e., "Slay the idolaters"). The definition of "Unbelievers" has been given a liberal interpretation by extremists.

Some conflicting verses regarding treatment and acceptance of Jews have caused immeasurable problems, and been used for excusing violence. But the Qur'an says little about the Jews. The Qur'an says to "Strike fear in God's enemy, but if the enemy is inclined toward peace, than you must be also, trust in God." It comes down to who is doing the interpretation and what purpose it needs to serve.

Unlike the Bible, Muhammad's original writings exist, documenting the accuracy of today's Qur'an. In another distinct difference from the Bible, it is forbidden to change one word or add commentary. But obviously, interpretation is fair game.

Islamic history is not an oasis of peace; "The House of Islam" and "House of Unbelief," later to take on the name "House of War," divide it. In Muhammad's time, wars to spread the "good fortune" of Islam were born. It was a policy of "convert or die," except for Jews and Christians who were allowed to retain and practice their faith. (The Jews lost their land, but could work it and pay taxes. Christians kept theirs and paid taxes.) Major battles occurred early with the Pagans in Mecca. Much like the American Civil War, it was brother against brother, father against son. Family was secondary compared to Islam.

Muhammad was an active participant in war and accompanied by the four original "Rightly Guided" Companions. He eventually conquered the Pagans and return to Mecca. There he took control of the large temple familiar today with thousands of faithful circling it like angels around God. The Ka'bah's famous "Black Stone" was believed part of the first worship alter built by Adam. The black rock was lost for many years after Noah's Flood, until Abraham received it from the angel Gabriel. Abraham and his son Ishmael (Mohammad's ancestor) reconstructed the Ka'bah and made the stone part of the structure. Over time the structure became a pagan temple, and would be damaged in battle and rebuilt many times.

For thirty years, Muhammad ruled the region, accompanied by the four Companions. Many battles occurred with territory and converts won for Islam. One particularly brutal battle at Badr caused the Muslims to change the direction they faced in prayer, from Jerusalem to Mecca. It was in this battle that Muhammad promised rewards in heaven to martyrs in battle. The promise was not quite the modernized, sexually charged rock-star fantasy that extremists use, but an inducement to charge and face death, knowing that God would welcome them to paradise. Martyrs were also expected to actually face their enemy and fight in those days, not strap on bombs and kill innocents.

Muhammad had been statesman, judge, general, and Prophet. At no time during his rule was there a question of leadership, or discord with the faith.

Upon his death, all that changed. Fraction occurred with the first successor. Some wanted an elected leader, while others wanted a Muhammad family member, or direct succession of rule. The first four successors were the "Rightly Guided" Companions. As Islam flourished, it was marred by corruption and nepotism. Three out of four of the Companions were assassinated. The last successor was Muhammad's son-in-law and nephew Ali. Ali had long been a confidant, and was considered fair and honest. But even he was considered an "unbeliever" by extreme elements that had surfaced, and he was murdered.

A split in Islam occurred over succession, with a newly named sect, Shi'a (Shi'ite), or "Followers," of Ali and family successors. The Sunnis believed in an elected Khalifah or caliph, meaning "successor," likely because that opened power-grabbing to everyone. Ali's son, Husayn, had been requested by the Shi'a to help in defending Karbala, but during battle the locals abandoned him. He was killed while holding his son in his arms. The victors beheaded Ali and displayed it.

Fervent Shi'a males still flog themselves on the anniversary of the battle as repentance during Ashura. The civil wars between the sects continued into the middle ages, until the Sunni finally emerged as the dominant sect.

The Sunni didn't want change, and approved of the social and political order under the caliphate. To the Sunni, obedience to authority was a divine command. Shi'a considered themselves as defenders of the oppressed, and to be against privilege. Their differences initially were small, but then grew into hatred and mistrust. Other sects, such as Wahhabi, teach that the Shi'a were invented by Jews, are liars, and not Muslims at all. The Shi'a followed, what they considered authentic rulers, Imams, meaning "in front of, or before." This term is loosely used in modern translation as the guy at the local mosque who leads prayers.

But the last real Imam mysteriously disappeared. He is now considered the "Hidden Imam" or Mahdi, who will return and bring justice and equity in a world of injustice. There were numerous Imams who fell to corruption, or were defeated in battle and glamorized as being betrayed, or labeled martyrs. There have also been false Mahdi, but little is said about them. But the recurring radical Islamist theme is one of denial, revenge, and the propensity to blame others.

For nearly a thousand years in world history, Muslims were a power to be feared. Once considered the "Orient," the Mideast had superior wealth, skill, and armies to those of Europe. Expansion of Muslim territory extended to what would be seventh-century Spain, Italy, North Africa, and Eastern Europe. With the conquests came the Islamic religion, which lives on today in parts of Spain, Eastern Europe and Russia. It was and still is a Muslim duty to share their good fortune of God's final revelation, and bring it to the world, if possible, by peaceful means.

However, Europe too had God's final revelation, and it fought back, though not all at once or right away. Europe was still barbaric in many ways, and poor. Europe was mostly Christian, and this presented a double challenge to the Muslims. They had to conquer and contain both religion and territory.

While other religions were allowed to exist in conquered lands, Muslim occupation was unacceptable to the Europeans, and that started the Crusades. One of the more absurd extremist accusations is calling the U.S. "Crusaders." First, America wasn't even on the map when the Crusades began; and second, the Crusades were a counter-attack to Islamic rule. The Muslims were the real first occupiers; the Crusades just meant to expel them. The "jihad" was to counter the counterattack. (By the way, jihad means "sacred struggle" or "strive," and is one of the five Islamic Pillars of Faith. It is literally meant as one's obligation in life to promote the faithful community, and defend against persecution and oppression. It is not meant to wage battle with peaceful people, and does not require violence. The new "Holy War" has perverted the meaning and reason of real jihad. But I digress.)

Europeans fought back, were repelled, yet they continued to fight on many fronts. Finally, in the eighth century, the Arabs were driven back from whence they came. The Crusades ultimately reached as far as Syria and down to Egypt. But that did not stop Islamic incursion. Among themselves, Shi'a and Sunni armies battled for control, heaping cruel treatment upon the loser. The religious capitol moved to Damascus to Baghdad and eventually Mecca. Alexander the Great responded to Greece being invaded by Persia (Iran), and set up the Byzantine Empire in victorious retaliation.

The Islamic world, unused to defeat, suffered additional invasions by Mongols, Tatars, and Turks. The Mongols would rule in Baghdad, but be converted to Islam before being overthrown. The Tatars were Islamic Turks who would temporarily control parts of Russia and Europe. The Turks eventually defeated the Byzantines in 1432 and started their own dynasty, the Ottoman Empire. The Sunni Ottoman Empire would bring prosperity and stability to the region for five hundred years.

The Muslim world ignored anything outside their sphere of influence. In their conquests they did not absorb arts, language, or culture. What the rest of the world knew was of no value, ungodly, and barbaric. They had the true faith and were superior because of that faith. But change was slowly occurring. During this time there had been robust trade between Europe and the Ottomans. Europe imported normal things like spices, tea and tobacco from Turkey. From Europe came increasingly sophisticated weapons and slaves. To protect shipping, the Europeans gained naval strength. The world's economic balance shifted with the infusion of wealth from the New World.

The Arab world was caught off guard as markets started disappearing, trade routes changed, and the European "barbarians" leaped beyond the once-dominant Muslim civilization. In a final push for world control, the Ottomans attacked and reached as far as Vienna before being beaten back. Yet, at the time, the defeat was considered just a delay in the world conversion to Islam. The Arab world was wrong, and Europe would become the occupiers.

By the eighteenth century (as the United States struggled to survive birth), blows to the Ottoman Empire reached as far as India and Southeast Asia. Colonial powers Britain, France, Holland, and Russia began to squeeze the empire from all directions. By the next century virtually the entire Islamic world was under the control or influence of the "Others." England colonialism reduced Islamic India to a shadow of itself, and sent missionaries into Africa and the Middle East, but the Christian culture was not embraced.

Current Islamic extremists' rhetoric revives and emphasizes the "Crusaders" and "Imperialists" labels, because Islamic forces inflicted great suffering on the unsuccessful Crusaders. The Imperialist label is used against the United States as well, even though the U.S.

had never forcefully occupied Arab soil, until Iraq. And even now, it is not with the intent to rule and dominate. (Sure we want to take their oil, but not their rule.)

Islamic propaganda counts on its students' ignorance of the Crusades as a response to the unprovoked attacks and occupation by Arabs, while the imperialism that followed was a defensive response to a continually hostile Islamic empire. This self-serving denial turns the various Islamic empires and conquests into historically oppressed victims. As the millennium of Islamic supremacy over other regions came to an end, these events were at odds with their conviction of faith.

As the one true religion, Islam could not be wrong, or God's people defeated in battle. It was not possible.

The Ottoman Empire's collapse was complete early in the twentieth century. Recurrent battles with the British and their tribal Arab allies forced the Ottomans to side with Germany in World War I. Arabs considered the ultimate defeat of the Ottomans as God's will. After the war, the conquering British carried out a bold "mandate" to establish a Jewish settlement in the divided empire. This would not be the last time Islamic regimes sided with Germany in war.

Out of the Arab tribal allies emerged a new leader, Ibn Sa'ud, from the family Al-Sa'ud. With humble beginnings commanding a network of bandits and wanderers, the Al-Sa'ud tribe steadily gained power over a vast region of worthless desert. Ibn Sa'ud cemented his control when he decidedly won a 1929 civil war. Brutality and oppression were Al-Sa'ud's hallmarks. The British rewarded their ally by giving him control over the land that would become Saudi

Arabia. In 1932, Ibn Sa'ud crowned himself "King," signaling his independence from colonial rule. And Saudi Arabia became the only country named after a living person.

In the early 1930s, as the Spanish Revolution captured the world's attention, the U.S. fell into Depression, Hitler began his rise to power, Stalin consolidated his control, and the British again promised Jewish colonization. And Standard Oil came to Saudi Arabia. Standard coveted the oil underneath the barren desert basically owned by Al-Sa'ud. Without his own means to extract the profitable crude, the king and the oil company created a partnership that survived wars, presidents, and negative publicity. Negative, for there is a hidden dark side to the Saudi regime.

World War II was close at hand and sides were being taken. Russia secretly entered into a partnership with the Axis powers to divide England's Middle East colonies and markets. Germany began actively pursuing Persia as an ally.

Persia had been a thorn in the side of the Sunni Ottomans for centuries as a rival to Islamic leadership. As Shi'a and not considered Arab, Persians were outsiders, and thereby hated by the Sunni dominated region. However, Persia was more culturally advanced in literature and the sciences (originating chess, Algebra, the stirrup, and most importantly, coffee-bean roasting). While Persia had undergone through numerous internal wars and been conquered by the Byzantines, it had never been defeated by the Ottomans.

Persia also made some other infamous contributions to history. An eleventh-century Persian order known as the "Assassins" began to torment and intimidate its enemies with a new kind of warfare. Primarily, the targets were enemy princes, generals, and the occasional unfortunate Crusader. With the killing often in full public view, these devotees did not expect to survive, since they were to make no attempt to escape and failure was a sin. They were to get close and kill only the carefully selected target in order to redeem their reward in paradise. Random slaughter was not accepted.

"Aryan," which means "Noble," was an ancient pre-Islamic ethnic culture in Persia and India. In Farsi, the language of Iran, "Iran" translates to "Land of the Aryans." The Aryan name was revived by the Third Reich, and applied for its own purposes to describe a superior race originating in the Nordic region. The nationalist revival was an attempt to persuade one "noble," superior, and different people to join with another. Hitler also employed another symbol from Persian/Indian culture, the swastika. On a light note, are current white supremacists unwittingly calling themselves Iranian? Anyway, back to Germany and the war.

The Nazis were looking for sympathetic, like-minded regimes in the area. Hitler needed help fighting English colonialism and the establishment of a Middle East Jewish settlement. German writers in the Middle East portrayed America as soulless and artificial, without the pure heritage of Germany and Iran. Germany was Iran's largest trade partner. Pro-Nazi sentiment quietly spread across the region, and had the support of religious leaders and the founder of the Muslim Brotherhood. In 1941 a pro-Nazi coup, with material and weapon backing from Germany, erupted against the pro-British government in Iraq. With Germany poised to open diplomatic ties with Iraq's new government, Russia (still a German ally from a 1939 pact) quickly recognized it first.

The British responded by overthrowing the coup in the Anglo-Iraqi War, and Iraq's leaders fled to Persia. Later in 1941, fearful of Iran's intent, England and Russia invaded and forced the abdication of the pro-German Shah. Flushed from hiding, Iraq's deposed leaders went to Europe under the protective custody of Axis powers.

In 1945, Roosevelt visited Al-Sa'ud to consider a Jewish settlement somewhere in Palestine. While that idea was rejected, the president was enticed into placing an air base right next to Aramco (Arab American Oil Company) headquarters. Even though Al-Sa'ud had become a trade ally, it did not prevent him from speaking anti-American rhetoric to the Islamic masses. Despite the king's bluster, Saudi oil enabled the Allies to continue and end the war. Saudi oil aided in the rebuilding of war-weary nations, and contributed to the emergence of a new, affluent, industrial superpower.

At the end of the war, Britain and France would see their regional domination replaced by the United States and the Soviet Union. The new world powers would allow Europe to be seen in a friendlier light by Arabs, no longer as conquerors or aggressors. There were now new Crusaders. Seizing on that distrust, the USSR promoted American "imperialistic" themes in their propaganda to the Arabs. The spread of Soviet communism to the Middle East was veiled as a "movement." The Russians argued that they had much in common with the Muslims: opposition to the West, democracy, and Jews—especially the formation of a Jewish state.

Prior to the British Mandate at the conclusion of World War I to create a Jewish state, no Palestinian state existed. For that matter, geographically Palestine was never a specific land. In history, Palestine was an evolving region, named in Hebrew for "Land of the Philistines." The Crusaders had called it the "Holy Land" and "Kingdom of Jerusalem." The idea of a Palestinian people being dislodged from a long-established homeland, or country, was false. Palestinians were, and continue to be the unwanted of Arab society, but more on that later. Worldwide sympathy followed the Holocaust survivors when the Jews were allowed to settle and establish Israel in 1948.

Still, many former, discreet pro-Nazi Arab regimes were uneasy about being discovered, and having Jews so close. The U.S. and USSR were pivotal influences in Israel's development at this time. The Russians were courting special favor at Israel's back door and selling arms through Czechoslovakia. These sales allowed Russia to play both sides of the Jewish debate without repercussions. The arms enabled Israel to repel and defeat Arab armies in a "welcome to the neighborhood" war. Saudi Arabia did not send troops into battle, only money. In winning the war, Israel dispelled some of its underdog, hapless-victim stigma in the court of world opinion. While the defeat was militarily stunning and humiliating to the Arab cause, it won the Arabic sympathy.

This was also the start of the Palestinian conflict. Then as now, the Palestinian refugees were not welcomed in other Arab countries. At the time,

Palestinians were actually forbidden to travel to certain Arab countries, since the Arabs did not want these poor, radical elements within their fragile new domains. The Palestinians weren't thrilled to be in young Israel, but lacking organization, they missed out on the final round of Middle East musical chairs.

The Arabs established a fund to support the Palestinians that included plenty of lip service. Importantly, the creation of a Jewish state within Arab country was considered an act of aggression; therefore to Arabs, any response was considered defensive. Likewise, any Israeli action was viewed as aggressive. Israel had the exact opposite view. The Jews had known annihilation, and would fight to survive.

Israel did not embrace the Russians, so the USSR moved its attention toward Syria, Egypt and Iran. In 1951, Iran nationalized British oil holdings. The 1952 Egyptian Revolution put Nasser in power, teaming him with Tito of Communist Yugoslavia. The Suez Canal was nationalized by Egypt in 1956, making Nasser, a secular nationalist, an Arab hero. The U.S. forced Britain, Israel and France to abandon war in the area over the canal. The thanks it got? Egypt, Syria, and Iraq turned to Russia for arms.

Within Egypt existed the small extremist group of the Muslim Brotherhood that condemned current Islam as corrupt, and in need of violent redemption. That path would require a cataclysmic battle with Jews and Christians. While suppressed by Nasser, the Brotherhood would emerge later to assassinate Anwar Sadat, and have al-Qaeda's Al-Zawahiri serve some time in prison for his complicity as a member. Also about this time in Syria and Iraq, a new socialist movement called the "Renaissance" party, or Ba'ath

Party, was beginning. The popularity of these secular movements and unrest was unsettling to Saudi Arabia.

During the English colonization period, the oil-rich emirate of Kuwait was created. In 1961, shortly after England relinquished its control, Iraq threatened invasion of the Sunni neighbor to the south over a standing Ottoman Empire boundary dispute. After being under Great Britain's protection for so many years, Kuwait had few military resources, but they had powerful friends to request help. England and Saudi Arabia sent troops, ships and aircraft to defend against any incursion by Iraq. The invasion never happened, and Iraq recognized Kuwaiti sovereignty two years later.

Created in 1964, the Palestinian Liberation Organization (PLO) was dedicated to establishing an independent state on the same territory as Israel. Although the Palestinian cause had not unified the Arabs, fashioned a government, or moved toward peace, the Russians and Chinese actively courted the PLO. In the Six Day War of 1967, Israel again defeated Egyptian, Syrian, and Jordanian forces. Likely a ploy to subdue Soviet Jews from any thoughts of rebellion, Russian propaganda equated Israel with the Nazis as aggressors, racists, and "invaders." The Palestinian territories of Golan Heights, Gaza Strip, Sinai Peninsula, and the West Bank, lands the Arab countries had once occupied, were now lost.

The defeated Arabs placed the fight solely in the hands of the PLO. Kind of, "Okay, we tried, it's your problem." A costly resolution to the Palestinian cause was not a goal of surrounding Arab monarchies; conversely the violence and bloodshed were a convenient sympathetic diversion to their own regimes' oppression and poverty.

The 1970s generated turmoil that could have set the Middle East on fire. "Black September" saw presidential assassination attempts, and spectacular PLO hijackings that escalated into a Jordanian civil war involving Syria, the United States, and Soviet Union. Egypt and Syria invaded the Sinai and Golan Heights in the Yom Kippur War with Israel. The Arab countries used Soviet weapons, while Israel had the backing of the English and French. Though the war resulted in a geographical stalemate, Israel and Egypt finally agreed in 1979 to Israeli withdrawal from the Sinai.

Stung by the Yom Kippur War defeat, Arabian Oil Producing Export Countries (OPEC) united for a yearlong oil embargo against those who had helped Israel. A conservative family member upset with King Faisal's modern reforms assassinated the third son of Saudi Arabia's founder. The assassin was eventually beheaded. Lebanon became embroiled in a fifteen-year civil war fueled by Christian and Muslim militias, and the PLO. Throughout the Mediterranean, Russia continued fanning anti-American sentiment in an effort to create instability and diffuse its influence.

This era witnessed the emergence of an Arabian middle class raised on oil wealth. Oil had caused class disparity, a noticeable gap between the poor and the wealthy. For the first time, most Arabs became aware of what the outside world had, and they didn't. Besides exporting oil, Arab countries did not have an industrial base and were dependent on everything. A new generation of Arabs was influenced by Western ideas through fashion, music, films and television. Now of age, young Muslims had too many dreams and too few opportunities. The frustrated, semi-educated poor were easy targets for the lurking extremists who blamed their woes on the West. The world would not have to wait long to bear witness to their prodigy.

In 1978, the Shah of Iran was overthrown in a brutal revolution that saw the exile of over 100,000 citizens, the confiscation of private property, trials and executions of ideologues and scholars, and repression—all in the name of God. Led by exiled Shi'a cleric Khomeini, Iran proclaimed to be restoring a true Islamic state. Angered by the decadence of the West, Khomeini also condemned the Wahhabis (ultra-conservative Sunni) and the Muslim Brotherhood for their views. Western culture was defined as an enemy that was subverting the Islamic community. Those at home who disagreed were "unbelievers" and importers of infidel ways. Khomeini also vowed to get rid of Jimmy Carter, the Shah, and Saddam before his death. He succeeded in two out of three.

Just as much anger was directed against Iran's loss of status. Once a great and powerful force, Iranians wanted respect and recognition. Had they not expelled the corrupt puppet regime of the Shah, faced down the "Great Satan" America, and struck fear in all the neighboring regimes? The nationalism revived by the Nazis and the superior "noble" race theme still echoed. The revolution also started a trend of attacking the U.S. (in this case an embassy) without retaliation. Carter's disastrous response cannot be counted as retaliation.

The title "Great Satan" is an honorary one, imposed on the world leader and power. As the leader, we are hated, and we are blamed no matter what. To those in America who want to be liked by everyone: Sorry, it'll never happen. Only if the United States gave up its civilization, freedoms, and leadership, and became irrelevant, would another power get the title and blame. America would still likely retain a "Little Satan" status, however.

In 1979, the USSR invaded Afghanistan after a communist coup. Refugees poured into Pakistan and began an anti-Soviet resistance. The U.S., trying to block Soviet expansion, started to train and arm the native freedom fighters. What the U.S. failed to recognize was a radical element in the mujahidin (sacred soldiers, or holy warriors). A group now called the "Afghan Arabs" had come to join in the battle against Islam. Afghans were not Arabs, so there was no cultural or family connection there. Regardless, Saudi Arabia and neighboring Arab countries encouraged their restless, unemployed, uneducated males to join in this jihad. Osama bin Laden was a fighter, though neither poor nor uneducated. Meantime, in Pakistan, the radical Wahhabi cult of Islam began the infiltration of the Madrasas (religious schools). Their efforts would generate additional fighters known as the "Students," or Taliban.

The Soviet defeat in Afghanistan glamorized Islamic war, and the image was irresistible to Islamic youth. Educated only with the Qur'an, the Taliban's archaic symbolism and language struck a nerve. While none of it was true, the tales of miracles in battle, fighters against huge odds, swords of angels, and close combat recalled the ancient glory of Muhammad's armies. Nowhere was there Islamic gratitude to America for furnishing weapons like Stinger missiles, or training sheep herders and poppy farmers to fight. Only when pressed, would the Afghan Arabs give very marginal credit to their benefactors who "showed up when the fight was over."

Afghanistan had only wanted liberation, and had initially rejected overtures from the Wahhabi cult. But as history would show, the Taliban would return, bringing Wahhabi discipline, and create a training ground for extremists. The U.S. would live to regret failing to recognize the emerging threat, and leaving Afghanistan to whoever wanted it. Our focus was China and Russia, not religious poppy farmers gone wild.

At the quiet urging of Saudi Arabia, the West supported Saddam Hussein's 1980 war against Iran. Calling Saddam "the Sword of Islam," the Saudis hoped for a victory over a Shi'a Islamic regime they viewed as a threat. The Saudis, being Wahhabi Sunni, had allowed Shi'a holy sites to be destroyed. The Americans were looking for disguised revenge. The Iraq-Iran war wasn't really about a major infraction, except that Saddam (a Sunni) had a big military, and feared the Shi'a revolution. He also reintroduced the art of using chemical weapons.

The nine-year war caused the exodus of over 100,000 Iraqis, and over one million casualties for the Iraq and Iran armies. Both sides emerged more powerful than before the war. The loser was the U.S., which would be criticized for supporting a brutal dictator that punished countrymen he felt were unsupportive or a threat.

Other important times:

In 1983, Hezbollah, the "Party of God," kills two hundred and forty-one Marines in Beirut.

In 1984, I turn thirty.

In 1989, Khomeini dies, leaving a will that's critical of puppet Islamic regimes, specifically pointing out Saudi Arabia for supporting the Wahhabi cult. We will get to the Wahhabis shortly.

Iraq turned its attention back to an earlier disputed prize, Kuwait. In 1991 Saddam invaded, quickly overpowering the tiny army, and horrifying the Arab world. The fabled mujahidin were nowhere to be found in Kuwait. Osama had called for the fighters to be allowed to defend the emirate, but was turned down by Saudi Arabia. Saddam's military was quickly pushed back across the border by a humiliating U.S. attack that saved Kuwait, and our oil interests.

As payment, the U.S. was allowed to (unfortunately) place and maintain bases on Saudi soil, to monitor the "No-Fly Zone" and protect the Saudis. This intrusion (or defilement) by unbelievers within the borders of Islamic holy land was more than many could tolerate. In addition, U.S. forces served as a constant reminder of Arab weakness and dependence on Western protection. These factors conflicted with Islamic teaching and history, and confused the frustrated Muslim youth.

The mujahidin searched for fights elsewhere. Moving to Somalia, Osama formed al-Qaeda, the "Base." The '90s provided easy targets and empty words, courtesy of the United States. In 1993, the first attack on the World Trade Center occurred. In 1995, the American Mission was bombed in Riyadh, Saudi Arabia. In 1996, the Kabar Towers were bombed in Saudi Arabia. In 1998, two U.S. Embassies bombed in East Africa. In 2000, the USS Cole was bombed in Yemen.

These acts of terrorism were not all al-Qaeda, but they came from the same source of extremism. What finally prompted an American response seemed to coincide more with adverse political news at home than retaliation or imminent danger abroad. A few lobbed Tomahawk missiles at Afghanistan proved harmless to the terrorists; more damage was done to Monica Lewinsky's dress.

As the United Nations impotently stood by and Europe fretted, the United States finally intervened in Bosnia and Chechnya. Despite promising that genocide would never again occur within its boundaries, Europe allowed the rape and murder of thousands of Muslims. Since Bosnians were European Shi'a, the Sunni-controlled Middle East criticism was subdued.

Despite the unselfish efforts of America, little positive recognition was given it by the Arab world. The unwelcome Afghan Arabs that showed up in Bosnia and Chechnya had no effect, and Osama claimed that the U.S. withheld arms from rebels that allowed for the massacre. While Osama spread falsehoods, counting on his followers' ignorance, his fighters were accused by the locals of torture, murder, and grave desecration (a Wahhabi trait). Hamas claimed that U.S. intervention in Bosnia to promote human rights was actually an effort to impose its influence in the region. Oh yeah, just what the United States needed, rocky farmland. Activists would be screaming "No blood for sheep!"

Absent was criticism of Russia, or China (and Iraq, Libya, or PLO), which supported Milosevic and blocked the UN. Besides, Arabs knew that it was more acceptable to criticize U.S. actions than Russian ones. The good news was Albania labeled Osama as "an enemy of civilization." Leading Bosnian Muslim clerics lauded the American response.

After 9/11, newspapers in the region carried headlines like Nobody veils the face of Liberty's face, and calling America Pride of this World. (Their support continues, as forces from that region are serving in the Coalition in Iraq.)

The insecurity the rest of the world had been living with finally came to our door. 9/11 changed America's perception of invincibility. And with it came the uneasy feeling of being hated, and killed for just being us. Of course, protesters and some media assumed that not being loved was our fault. That is egotistical and ridiculous. These countries and factions are perfectly capable of hating us on their own.

So who are the mujahidin and the Wahhabi, and what do they want? Put simply, they are violent religious fanatics, and they want America and what it stands for gone from the face of the planet.

The sacred-fighters concept dates back to Muhammad's warriors defending Islam on the battlefield. Many Muslims are offended by today's self-appointed executioners taking the name associated with those who fought in real wars against actual, not contrived, oppressors. Unfortunately, the average, peaceful Muslim is unable, or afraid, to criticize extremism. Moderate clerics are also reluctant to take a stand and risk death.

Modern extremists are indoctrinated at an early age. They learn little else but reciting the Qur'an and Wahhabi interpretation in Madrasas. These fanatic factories have a head start on the war on terrorism. After World War II, it was estimated that 80 percent of

Islamic elementary schools were Wahhabi. Between 1980 and 2000, the number of Madrasas in India surpassed the total built in eight centuries.

Today, students are "encouraged" to participate only in approved religious activities, nothing social. Teachers and clerics fabricate history to fit their purpose, since the students almost certainly won't question religious instruction. The use of ancient terms conjures up gallant images of the Islamic glory days. The Qur'an is taken out of context with self-serving interpretations, such as the West as the reason for Islam's world decline and humiliation. The message that Western influence is the root of problems diverts attention away from internal Arabic-regime problems and contradictions.

These impressionable Madrasa youth are taught it is preferable to leave this miserable life, die for Islam, and proceed to heaven to receive God's reward. They are not taught to dream of this life, but of paradise, their heavenly wife, and immortality should they die in battle. Socially inept, narrow minded, and constantly reminded they have no future, it is not surprising these angry young men look to death.

It is difficult for most people to imagine dying for religion. While we can understand sacrificing for our family or country, due to the nature and fullness of our lives, religion is generally not a top priority on the "to die for" list. But to Muslims, faith is the basis of their being, it is order, the law, it tells them how to live. Traditional Muslims can coexist in world society, while extremists live within the black-and-white world of "House of Islam" and House of Unbelief."

We have all witnessed the Islamic reactions to the cartoons of Muhammad, and Pope Benedict XVI's speech where he supposedly disrespected the Muslim faith. Americans are insulted all the time, so what's the big deal? Conservative Muslims do not consider other religions and cultures legitimate therefore, criticism is acceptable.

So, what caused this modern extremism? We have to go back again, and finally explain the Wahhabi.

Remember, upon Muhammad's death, challenges to a successor and the path of Islam occurred. Extreme elements preached separatism and fundamentalism, and called any opposition "unbelievers." In the following centuries there were other challenges, each growing stronger, until they were defeated, only to reemerge.

In the 1700s, Wahhab, a poor, uneducated man frustrated by his place in life after visiting fabled cities with caravans, declared that all Muslims had fallen into disbelief. Wahhab's envy created the disdain for that which he did not have. Even today, apocalyptic messages from the fringe seem to draw a disenfranchised element of society, and this was no different. Wahhab found others who hated and were jealous as well. Wahhab dictated there should be no reverence for the dead (recall the grave-desecration accusations in Bosnia), including visiting Muhammad's tomb. He also decreed no shaving, no graven images (like the Buddhist statues destroyed in Afghanistan by the Taliban), and that all who didn't follow him should be killed, their possessions taken, and their wives and daughters violated. Wahhab's unbending version of Islam should stand alone, with all other beliefs destroyed, including the Shi'a.

Wahhab visualized himself on an equal footing with the Prophet Muhammad, perhaps more so, since he reinterpreted, and knew, what God's "recitation" really meant. Devotion became an absolute and rigid following of doctrine, without understanding or compassion. Interestingly, Muhammad had predicted centuries earlier that from Wahhab's birthplace in Najd would come "the horns of Satan." Perhaps by chance, twelve of the fifteen Saudis involved in 9/11 were also from this region.

When the Ottomans ordered the radical Wahhab arrested, he fled and found refuge with another rebel, bandit Muhammad ibn Sa'ud (patriarch of the Al Sa'ud family). The two outcasts bonded and formed a crude "government" based on inherited power. One acted as the sword and the other the mouth. Their families intermarried in order to preserve the family succession. By their deaths in the late 1700s, they ruled most of the Arab peninsula.

In the 1800s the Wahhabi sect spread its toxic influence to India and Pakistan, causing conflict where there had been none. The descendants of Wahhab and Sa'ud carried the new movement to brutal heights, attacking the Holy City of Karbala (Iraq), slaughtering thousands, and desecrating the grave of Muhammad's son-in-law Husayn. The Al-Sa'ud Wahhab raiding party proceeded to Medina, boldly looting Muhammad's tomb and destroying Companion's graves. In Mecca, they killed women and children, destroyed all shrines, and covered the Ka'bah in black. The Ka'bah had traditionally been covered in the regal colors of whoever had regional sovereignty; black is an indication the site is still controlled by the Wahhabis.

Several attempts were made by the Ottomans to restrain this movement, but none had long-lasting success. Though briefly expelled from the region, Al-

Sa'ud returned retaking lands and power. In 1924, he repeated the atrocities in Medina, this time leveling the Prophet's house and family graves. Al-Sa'ud also expelled the family of direct descendants of Mohammad. The Arab world protested, but nothing was actually done. (Mohammad-era heritage sites continue to be destroyed for Saudi commercial and tourist-related construction projects). Over the coming decades, incredible wealth and privilege would come to the house of Al-Sa'ud, providing funding and cover for the Wahhabi brand of terrorism. (After 9/11, Israel intercepted documents proving Saudi Arabian complicity in funding terrorism. Saudi lobbyists quickly quieted the issue.) The leader of the Iranian Revolution, Ayatollah Khomeini, accused Wahhabis of distorting the Qur'an, being a cult, and having "devilish ends."

The most infamous modern Wahhabi was, of course, Osama bin Laden. Seen as forsaking a life of privilege to face hardship and danger, bin Laden was viewed as a hero, a leader who faced and defeated Satan, killing more infidels than anyone before. Bin Laden's diatribes were filled with glorified historical misrepresentations that stoked perverse mujahidin anger. Like other terrorist leaders, he had no problem calling for others to become martyrs, while never placing himself in danger. Osama repeatedly called for the death of America because of its intrusion on Muslim holy land. Naturally, he avoided criticizing his Saudi benefactors for permitting infidel entry in the first place.

From Arab slums the hopeless young flock to the front lines of what they perceive, or have been told, is a Holy War. Drawn by heroic imagery and the desire to vent fury, they readily, almost eagerly, look for the opportunity to become martyrs. These fighters will not accept compromise, only death or victory. Either way, they win. There can be no goodwill toward an enemy of God. And since they have decided that God needs their help, they will do what it takes. To them, until the world is under strict Islamic control, there will be endless, ever-escalating warfare. It will be the ultimate triumph of good over evil, of God over the ungodly.

In the real world, these fighters have no hope, no social skills, and no future. For the most part, they are just programmed robots that do not fit in, or relate to the modern world. In jihad, they are part of something with others of their kind. They can take revenge on a world that has forsaken them, that has things they don't understand, and can't have. They can tell themselves: If it is not of Islam, it is not of God. If God did not give it to them, it must be evil. The random slaughter of innocents, forbidden in traditional Islam, is excused as "God's will," and what apologists refer to as "involuntary martyrs." Since worldly life means nothing to them, they don't care about anyone else's.

Suicide is specifically forbidden in Islam, so is conveniently termed "martyrdom." The wording used by these fighters, including Zawahiri, reveals antiquated verbiage from their Qur'an instruction. Just listen to any terrorist statement and they are still referencing swords, slaying, and evildoers; they end up sounding like they were educated on Dungeons and Dragons.

The terrorists are products of years of corrupt and tyrannical Arab regimes often supported by the West. The moral and economic hypocrisy in their native countries is more often than not blamed on the West, i.e., "the Devil made us do it." Freedoms are strictly regulated within most Islamic countries. Only certain protests are allowed, and often encouraged to provide relief to the boiling pot, to keep the anger turned outward. (Have you ever wondered where all the burning U.S. flags and signs come from?) Almost never is criticism of the ruling government allowed. News of the outside world is strictly censored, so most citizens depend on the mosque to provide what they need to know, and how to think about it, and the government is happy to provide that version of reality.

It doesn't matter what U.S. policy has done, is doing, or will do; envious countries will continue to hate us, and use us, and we will let them. The promise of Wahhabi Islamic superiority is impossible to resolve with a country like America. So America must be brought down. We are a land of plenty and freedoms unknown to most of the world. The seduction of liberty is what radical Islam fears most, because despite their efforts, it is too late to block democratic imagery. Backwards religious extremists who want to return to tribal days will ultimately have to battle with modern thinking within their borders.

To prevent calls for democratic governments, improved standards of living, and freedoms, Arabic leaders in Saudi Arabia and Syria barely survive in a mixture of piety, perversion, terrorism, and repression. At some time, the Al-Sa'uds will have to explain their obscene wealth and the moral decay of the privileged ruling class to an internal jihad; until then the Saudi monarchy will fund distractions elsewhere. Arabs will not allow peace with Israel, or true democracy in the Middle East to take hold. They need conflict to feed the beast they have created.

So will democracy work in Iraq? It depends on how badly Iraqis want it, and are willing to stop the sectarian violence. Democracy is said to be the most difficult form of government to establish, and the most difficult to destroy. Our own early government struggled for years under intrigue, bribery, and selfish interests, and—I'm being sarcastic here—look how far we've come.

In the past, American and British-influenced countries modeled their new governments after their benefactor. Some like Iran have taken an odd mixture of both, with a president and constitution, a parliament and Prime Minister. Iraq has followed in that respect. However, Iran is not a democracy, but a theocracy with the elected government answerable to a supreme religious council. There is no separation of church and state. On that topic, indicating the dangers of a religious state, Thomas Jefferson re-coined a familiar phrase and wrote, "Divided we stand, united we fall."

The unique problem in this culture is the internal hatred among the believers. There is no consensus or common goal. The Sunni despise the Shi'a, yet the Sunni are not strict enough for the Wahhabi. Even within their sects, loyalty comes down to tribes, families, and neighborhoods. Citizens can't count on the police or army to be immune from exercising sectarian revenge. Revenge is a centuries-old part of Arab culture. A Sunni might kill any Shi'a for some perceived injustice, followed by a multiplied reciprocation spreading like a cancer. Opposing sects will together fight a common enemy, until resuming the older battle—a battle with no reason or conclusion.

So, might there be eventual peace in the region? Probably not. And the Iraqi form of government will likely end up something different than what is in place, mainly because it isn't working. The Saudis won't want Iraq to become a Shi'a-dominated regime, and Iran is not going to want a working democracy next to them. We have two choices. We can help make Iraq somewhat relatively stable and get the heck out before the sectarian explosion.

Or, since Arab culture respects and fears strength and power, we can get tough and become as brutal with the insurgency as they are with us. We can also start pressuring our Arab "friends" to get out of the shadows, get involved, and stop funding the violence. Otherwise, without a strong hand and regional support, we can't, and shouldn't, protect Iraq from what will eventually come back to haunt that part of the world.

PHOTO ARCHIVE

Bombed cars are a common sight along Baghdad streets. (DL)

What grass? (DL)

Mural inside the Republican Palace depicting missiles firing towards Iran. (DL)

A sand storm envelopes Baghdad with talcum-like dust. (Andy Stefanek)

Typical Duck and Cover bunkers don't inspire confidence in surviving a rocket attack. (Denn Pietro)

During the holidays, the dining staff tries hard to create a festive atmosphere. These mutant reindeer are the result. (DL)

When two members of our crew get married, this is their wedding cake box. This kid must be the baker's son. (DL)

The defendants' holding cells. Saddam's is at the far end. Guards and cameras monitor their every move. (Andy Stefanek)

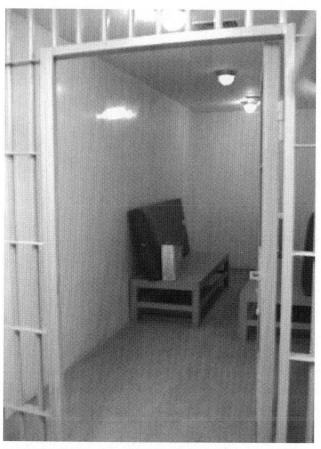

Saddam's courthouse holding cell. A far cry from his opulent palaces. (Mitchell Pietz)

The main entrance to the IHT court and former Ba'ath Party headquarters. (Denn Pietro)

The court's witness podium sits just feet away from the defendant's cage and Saddam's glare. (DL)

Up close and personal travel aboard a C-130 transport. It's hot, stuffy, and people are airsick. (Mitchell Pietz)

Saddam's Republican Palace pool. During hot days it is filled with sunburnt soldiers, and at night the place for karaoke and movies. (DL)

Even when getting a tan at Liberty Pool, soldiers can never be far from their weapons. (Andy Stefanek)

Thousands of Iranian helmets from the Iran-Iraq War spill down the base of the Crossed Swords monument. (DL)

President Bush walks among soldiers following his surprise embassy speech. (Andy Stefanek)

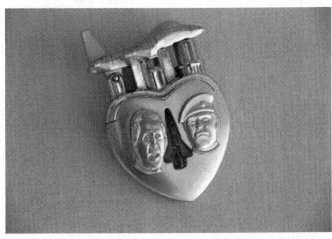

I purchased this Bush and Hussein lighter that flashes and makes a whistling dropping bomb sound. (DL)

*Authentic Iraqi police gear purchased from a street
vendor near the Crossed Swords. (DL)*

*Saddam's half-brother Barzan Ibrahim al-Tikriti sulks
on the courtroom floor while wearing long underwear.
(Desert Sky Media)*

The result of a mortar's direct hit on a residential trailer. (Andy Stefanek)

Awad Hamad al-Bandar (Dr. Evil) listens as the judge issues a verdict of death. (Desert Sky Media)

Saddam Hussein doesn't like receiving the death penalty one bit. (Desert Sky Media)

Acknowledgements

This story was composed using personal recollections, conversations, emails, and a daily journal written during the trial. A book form would have not been possible without additional research utilizing a myriad of archival sources for legal, historical, and cultural clarity.

Several Bernard Lewis works were an inspiration during my time in Iraq, and made me want to learn more. Books by Michael J. Kelly, Ali Allawi, Rajiv Chandrasekaran, Stephen Swartz, and Edward W. Said provided additional background, and deserve special mention. An excellent, factual account of the trials, "Enemy of the State," by Michael A. Newton and Michael P. Scharf, proved an invaluable resource to cross-reference time frames, and confirm personal notes.

Excerpt from "Abraham Lincoln" by Benjamin P. Thomas used with permission.

Photographs by Andy Stefanek, Denn Pietro, Mitchell Pietz, and Desert Sky Media used with permission. Thank you Scott and Dan for making your collections available.

Edited by Jim Thomsen. Thank you for your efforts and enthusiasm.

Thank you to the Iraqi nationals with the Regime Crimes Liaison's Office who offered so much of their time sharing stories, personal insights, and educating me. Asallam Alaikum.

Made in the USA
San Bernardino, CA
14 July 2017